Relationship Roulette

Relationship Roulette

Improve Your Odds at Lasting Love

CAROL DIAMOND

 PRAEGER

AN IMPRINT OF ABC-CLIO, LLC
Santa Barbara, California • Denver, Colorado • Oxford, England

Library of Congress Cataloging-in-Publication Data

Diamond, Carol.
   Relationship roulette : improve your odds at lasting love / Carol Diamond.
      p. cm.
   Includes bibliographical references and index.
   978–0–313–38357–1 (hard copy : alk. paper) — 978–0–313–38358–8 (ebook)
1. Mate selection. 2. Man woman relationships. I. Title.
HQ801.D5285   2010
646.7′7—dc22   2009050892

ISBN: 978–0–313–38357–1
EISBN: 978–0–313–38358–8

14 13 12 11 10   1 2 3 4 5

This book is also available on the World Wide Web as an eBook.
Visit www.abc-clio.com for details.

Praeger
An Imprint of ABC-CLIO, LLC

ABC-CLIO, LLC
130 Cremona Drive, P.O. Box 1911
Santa Barbara, California 93116-1911

This book is printed on acid-free paper ∞

Manufactured in the United States of America

To My Husband, Jim

Contents

Preface

It didn't dawn on me to write this book until I prepared a seminar about relationships, which was a result of 25 years of psychotherapy practice listening to so many people who had difficulty with relationships—wanting to be in one, wanting to get out of one, wanting to find the right one, wanting to stop choosing the wrong one. Then, prior to writing this book, I decided to systematically ask a random sample of people if they had a history of choosing the wrong partner, and if so, whether they ever noticed that they did this wrong—choosing repetitively. And even though I was amazed at amassing so many similar answers from people, I was not actually surprised to see that these people admitted to the peculiar experience they had finding themselves again and again making the wrong choice.

"That's me, where can I buy the book," is more or less the direct response I would get. Apparently, they all wanted to read a book—that was not yet written!

That was my mandate. That is, I knew I had to write this book, because the need to know about the nature of relationships was what people were keenly interested in. And because of my quarter of a century of training and experience in the field of relationship building, I knew what the questions were and I wanted to offer the reader my entire catalogue of revelations regarding the blind alleys of relationships as well as the better road to take when selecting a partner. In other words, I wanted my readers of this book to understand how and why they were repeating the same patterns over and over. I wanted them to learn new concepts and to gain knowledge and insight into their behavior.

I decided to present many case studies, as I knew my readers would find themselves in these illustrations by identifying with others just like themselves. I wanted the book to cover it all in order to vastly increase the probability that people would be better able, as a result of consulting this book, to choose better and to possibly make productive changes in the relationships they were already in.

It is not a coincidence that people keep failing into the same relationship traps. They know something is wrong but it becomes easier to be in denial than to look at the obvious: how miserable they feel in their relationship; how miserable they felt in most of their relationships, and, in the end, blaming themselves for such relationship failures.

So this book, *Relationship Roulette: Improve Your Odds at Lasting Love* is finally here to help the reader understand many things about the nature of relationships, not the least of which is what's known as the "repetition compulsion"—that people have the compelling feeling that brings them to repeat the same choices. With such choices, most people feel that they might be able to finally solve their problem. Of course, choosing the wrong person out of the same repetitive reflex never works. People need to begin by recognizing their own unhealthy patterns; that is, attachments they make to people who are not emotionally available or not really able to commit to a relationship—and they need to know the underlying reasons for their attraction to the same types of people.

This book looks at one's original family, which in some cases include parents who were not capable of providing the necessary love it takes to love and be loved. In other cases, even though the parents may have been available, they most likely had difficulty expressing their emotions. Such an analysis in the book shows how family dynamics are crucial to the way people related in their childhood and then have carried those same dynamics with them into adulthood. This is the crucial point that also relates to the beliefs learned early on, and how these beliefs dominate one's adult life. As some point, such beliefs may need to be challenged, and the case studies in the book reveal how this challenge can be accomplished. Thus, *Relationship Roulette* is an attempt to help readers recognize possible destructive patterns in order to understand the feelings involved in these patterns and how such patterns affect any relationship.

The reader can benefit by reading this book, as it will take you through a psychological journey of understanding how and why you are alone or how and why you're in a "bad" relationship. The book also can guide you to make the necessary changes for a more healthy relationship that will endure—a relationship that will be in your best interest.

Wouldn't you say it's better to choose wisely in contrast to constantly playing relationship roulette? The answer we believe is a resounding Yes!

Acknowledgments

My deepest appreciation to Dr. Henry Kellerman, friend and colleague, for providing the inspiration and encouragement I needed to write this book. He lived through the writing of the book with me providing emotional support, valuable contributions but most of all helping me to believe in myself.

I want to thank my very dear friend Sandy Ciccone who provided invaluable assistance in her help editing and contributing to the book along with her continued love and support.

To my Mom for her wisdom, judgment, encouragement and love over many decades.

I want to thank my husband, Jim, who stood by me, providing guidance and help in editing the book. I couldn't have written this book without his support and unconditional love.

I also want to thank my patients in my 25 years of private practice who have become the case studies used in the book.

Introduction

Jennifer literally loses herself in every relationship she has. After his divorce, Brian dates but keeps a distance between himself and his girl-friends. Neil lives vicariously through Linda, so he doesn't have to deal with his own emotions.

What do these men and women—some of the people studied in the case histories—have in common?

Like many of us, they seek out dates and relationships only to play old tapes from past failed relationships over and over again. We may choose partners as "fixer-uppers" and try to right all the wrongs we had in our childhood relationships. What many of us probably don't realize is that unless we recognize and work through emotional and behavioral issues from our families of origin, relationship disasters will not end.

Relationship Roulette is designed to help those who feel stuck—unable to achieve a lasting, loving relationship—to move on and make new choices by confronting and dealing with the old problems.

Jennifer, cited in the first example above, most likely did not have parents who unconditionally loved her and made her feel special. Did your parents make you feel special? Brian's parents probably kept emotional distance from their kids. Were your parents emotionally available to you? And Neil, well, he's the product of a narcissistic single mom who always insisted upon being the center of attention. Did your parents value you, and allow you to sometimes be the center of attention?

Unconsciously, some women keep going for the "bad boy" type only to see their worlds turned upside down when the bad boys dump them. Others are turned on by men who make them feel uncomfortable and inadequate. Those men eventually become bored and just vanish. Yet these same women claim to be bored by men who genuinely like them and make them feel at ease.

Why do women fall for men who may seem wonderful, but once committed appear to have changed from Dr. Jeckyl into Mr. Hyde? Do you do this? Is this you?

Wait a minute!

Before you defensively scream "no," think back over your dates, partners, and marriages. Most of us repeat patterns from the families we were raised in without being aware of it.

The woman who picks a man who's unavailable or who treats her badly most likely was treated badly by her parents, or they were not emotionally or physically available to her. The man who chooses a woman so he can help her may need to help himself first. Admit it—your parents weren't perfect. The people from our pasts that we are still trying to fix are usually parents. When a love interest comes into the picture, Jennifer and all the others like her still try subconsciously to fix the old stuff with their parents. In trying to fix or train a partner, what we're really trying to do is to fix our parents or families.

Unhealthy patterns can go on for years. People will stay with someone a long time thinking they can fix or change them. But until the Jennifers and Brians of the world let go and understand the dynamics of the past, healthy relationships won't be in their cards for the future.

Unless Jennifer gets help, she'll pick someone else who's unavailable or not good for her. Her partner also could fall in love with a woman who's not good for him. We seem to think that we can make people who cannot give love be able to give love. Or people who are abusive not to abuse. Or people who are not physically demonstrative more affectionate. Or people who are not emotional to communicate and share their feelings.

Why can't we quit playing "Relationship Roulette"? We start out with good intentions to find the perfect partner. Then it happens! We hit on a lucky number and think we've found our soul mate. Relationships seem to always start out great with happy anticipation for a bright future. We might think, "This is it." But then we realize we are playing the same game of pure chance and speculation again, and we ask ourselves, "How did we get here?"

Many of us will go after people to fix until we receive help or until we recognize and understand where the destructive patterns are

coming from and embrace change. This book will help you understand where you fit into the relationship game based upon your past
behaviors. Read the case studies carefully to see if you identify with
the men or women.

Sure, we're jaded. We've been there, done that. Experiencing and
hearing about so many failed relationships from coworkers, friends,
and family members make us skeptical about whether relationships
can work. We are afraid to roll the dice again.

Too many hurts, too much rejection, and repetitious disappointments can leave us ambivalent. When we do start with a new partner
and begin to invest our hearts, we gradually realize that the relationship is not making us happy. We wonder why. We think back—trying
to understand what went wrong. We may feel it was our fault.

Think back to when you were a child and thought you did something wrong that caused the hurt and rejection you felt. What did
you experience? Who hurt you when you tried to love them? You
may not remember feeling that it was your fault in the past. Without
resolution of the old hurts, old patterns repeat.

If you experience pain and rejection in the present with great inten-
sity, you probably felt similar feelings as a child. Investing too much in
most of your relationships may set you up for feeling anxious and
depressed when the relationship ends. This can make you angry and
frustrated—feeling like you don't want to try again. You can become
wary about banking on anyone.

Disappointment sets in. Somehow you felt you had the power to
make a new one work. But those thoughts can be destructive. You
may lose perspective, feeling you could have changed the outcome.
You contract a case of the "if onlys" or "what ifs." You probably have
no idea why your partner really ended it.

However, you may not have the knowledge or insight to understand
what happened. Your focus is only on how you felt and how you might
have been able to change things. Remember that lots of people have
disastrous relationships. You are not alone.

Building a good relationship is challenging. Without understanding
the challenges at hand and having the skills to make it work, relationships can be shaky. Making a relationship work takes two.

Relationship Roulette will help you understand how to change your
choice of partners, so those choices don't always lead to the same rot-
ten luck. You will begin to recognize and to understand your own personality or how you operate, how your partner operates, and the

dynamic interaction between you and your partner that can either make or break the relationship.

This book offers greater insight into thinking and behavior. It provides the necessary skills for productive ways of relating, so you can achieve the loving, lasting relationship you want and need.

CHAPTER 1

Choosing a Partner
Is Risky Business

When she locked eyes with Michael at a party, Jennifer was instantly attracted and tingled from head to toe. When you first see someone, you probably don't question your attraction—either you feel the chemistry or you don't.

INITIAL ATTRACTION

Most people are initially attracted by physical appearance. Some people look for specific qualities or features. It may be a person's smile, their eyes, or their hair—but something definitely attracts you and makes you want to get to know this person. You may not be interested in physical features but other attributes. You may find a person with a great sense of humor who makes you laugh even when you weren't feeling so hot. You may find a person whose caring nurturing ways draw you in. You may find a person who is financially successful. He or she may be intelligent or have a high level of status through his or her profession. Physical attributes may be easy to overlook when you find out what this person has to offer.

Men tend to be more attracted to the physical. A man will see someone, like the way she looks and want to meet her. However, as often happens after a while, the physical attraction may change. Some men choose a partner whose body type may not be their ideal. But as the relationship develops, body type becomes less important. You could also be in a relationship with someone who isn't your "dream" person and you may wonder why this happened.

THE BASIS OF ATTRACTION

The initial, electrifying chemistry is what appeals to most. Yet the important point is that getting to know someone brings more into the picture—such as qualities like those in someone else you knew and loved. The person may seem familiar to you, as if you had known them much longer than you have. You may even attribute qualities to them that they don't have. Some of this may be at a conscious level and some may be on an unconscious level.

Sometimes these automatic or unconscious processes can overpower what appears to be choosing a partner based on the initial attraction. Since the focus of this book is to have a more fulfilling relationship, and because the initial attraction may be influenced by other factors, we will focus on those areas that may be causing you problems so that making changes becomes a positive process.

The two examples or case studies that follow reveal how an initial attraction can be influenced by chemistry as well as learned behaviors. It may help you recognize that your attraction to someone may be the result of past experiences. It will also demonstrate how these past experiences can lead to unhealthy repetitive patterns when it comes to choosing partners.

JENNIFER AND MICHAEL

Jennifer, age 29, noticed Michael at a party. She had never seen him before. But from across the room she felt something inside that made her desperately want to meet him. She introduced herself and found him charming and nice. He seemed very interested, took her phone number, and told her he would call.

Jennifer couldn't sleep that night, because she was excited about the possibility of seeing him again. She said she felt like she was "already in love." Jennifer and Michael dated for about four months. During that time, Jennifer found herself spending a great deal of time thinking about the relationship and waiting for his calls. Since she felt somewhat intimidated by Michael, she allowed him to make all the moves. Many times, she felt uneasy and couldn't be herself. She noticed that she didn't feel free to say and do what she wanted. For Jennifer, being herself with Michael made her feel vulnerable and open to rejection. The ultimate fear was that Michael would leave her.

Instead of being herself, Jennifer behaved in a way that she thought would please Michael. However, this was all coming from Jennifer not Michael. Maybe Jennifer was picking up some feelings from Michael that led her to behave this way—feelings she was not aware of but had experienced in the past? Yet she thought she was happy. And in fact, they had some great times together. She even felt they were meant for each other, and she wanted to marry Michael—even in the face of her more-than-occasional discomfort. She thought she was happy just because she had a relationship and some sense of belonging.

Then it happened. After about four months, Michael stopped calling. Jennifer couldn't understand why. Nothing happened that she could think of that would stop him from calling. She called him and sensed that he seemed different. He was cold. He said things had gotten so busy at work that he needed some time alone, and added that he would call her soon. He never did.

Jennifer felt desperate. She had trouble sleeping, and thought about the relationship most of the time. She felt abandoned and depressed. She knew her tension level was having a negative effect on her work as well as on her other relationships. But she felt she was somehow at fault. Had she done something wrong so that he no longer wanted to be with her?

All she could think of was ways to get him back. She could not let go and move on. It was too painful for her to even think about not being with him. She obsessed about Michael most of the time.

Jennifer could have done some things differently. She could have asked herself what she needed from Michael instead of keeping her needs on hold from the beginning of the relationship. Apparently, her fear of losing her partner was so great that by default, she gave him all the power in the relationship. When the relationship ended, more important than the loss of Michael, was that Jennifer lost herself.

REPETITIOUS AND SELF-DEFEATING BEHAVIOR

Interestingly enough, this pattern was old news to Jennifer. In the past, she had several relationships that began and ended in the same way. In each, she felt that her partner was going to be different and not like the others. And she was right. They were all different, and yet the relationships always ended.

If she had understood her own history, she would have known each boyfriend was unavailable from the beginning. Insight and understanding allows the letting go to happen much sooner. If she works on it, the next time she becomes involved in a similar relationship, she can let go sooner and get out of it. Then the goal would be for her to not become involved in any more dead-end relationships.

Ironically, Jennifer did have some short-term relationships with men who were actually interested in having longer-term relationships. In fact, she felt very comfortable with these men, had no anxiety, and was able to be herself. Furthermore, these relationships did not stimulate her insecurities. However, Jennifer's biggest complaint about all of these men was that they were boring. She felt no chemistry. In fact, she said she actually felt suffocated by their attentive behaviors. The result was that Jennifer would eventually end these relationships.

Thus, instead of recognizing her self-defeating patterns, Jennifer kept repeating them. Her antennas were finely tuned to the wrong frequency. She would always end up feeling lonely, frustrated, and angry.

Jennifer's father was emotionally unavailable, which meant that he could not meet her emotional needs for love, attention, and nurturing. She was drawn toward that type of man, and her pattern was to try and "fix" him.

It's best to recognize after enough of these relationships that go nowhere that you have a problem. If you can't do it by yourself, you go to a therapist. That person can help you recognize and identify where the negative pattern originated. Jennifer's goal was to learn to give one of the men who were available a chance.

BOB AND KATHY ... AND DIANE

Bob, a divorced man of 46, had experienced several long-term relationships. In his early twenties, he married a woman who had one child from a previous marriage. While attending law school, Bob owned and ran a pub where Kathy tended bar. They worked well together, business was good, and they began to see each other romantically. After they married, Bob discovered that Kathy had substance abuse issues. A short time later, Kathy's use of drugs and alcohol began to interfere with their marriage. This problem also affected Kathy's four-year-old daughter. To complicate matters even more, Kathy and Bob had their own child. After about two years, Kathy decided to leave the marriage.

Bob loved Kathy and wanted the marriage to survive. He thought he would be able to help solve her problems. However, Kathy persisted with her plan for divorce. She planned to move out of state with her daughter. She felt she could not care for two children.

Bob was going to have to bring up their youngest daughter himself, and he did just that. He closed the pub and cared for his daughter while finishing law school. He graduated first in his class.

Some years later, Bob met Diane. She was a bright woman and a college professor. She had never married, but had a child from a previous relationship. Bob and Diane dated for about two years and then became engaged. Diane also wanted another child and got pregnant before she and Bob married.

Then she decided she didn't want to marry Bob after all. She just wanted to be friends and wanted Bob to have a large role in their daughter's life. Bob was in love with Diane and would not accept the fact that Diane no longer loved him in the same way.

Bob spent the next five years doing everything for Diane and their child, always with the hope that he could win back her love. During this period he didn't date anyone else, and he believed that they would indeed ultimately be back together. He wouldn't face his belief that this probably wouldn't happen, but he wasn't able to let go.

In the meantime, and quickly, Diane met someone else to marry. Bob became extremely depressed, was in shock, and sought help. His depression lasted for two years and only lifted when he was truly able to accept the loss of Diane and further, when he was able to give up his fantasy.

Bob then moved on to other relationships. But he began to develop a pattern that looked similar to the one he had with his wife Kathy. First, he found that he was attracted to younger women, and second, these younger women were those who had more emotional problems than he was consciously aware of or willing to acknowledge. However, since Bob was a very giving person, he chose to stay in these relationships, believing that he could "fix" these women or make them healthier.

Bob got to a point where he was not taking care of his own needs. It almost appeared that he had no needs except the need to keep his partner. He became enmeshed in his partner's issues and took the role of the "good daddy." That role was to be the "father" who was available and could meet all of his partner's needs. Bob was not consciously aware that he needed to keep his partner dependent so that she would not leave him.

However, Bob was really just as dependent on his partner. He was not aware that it was possible to have a partner who was actually separate and healthy. Or, perhaps he didn't feel he deserved someone who would want to, or could meet the needs he had so long suppressed. Taking this a step further, it was possible that, at this time, Bob was not even capable of being in a healthy, intimate relationship.

So, Bob has never had the kind of relationship he's wanted. He has been lonely and depressed, but unwilling to seek professional help. Bob needs help in recognizing and understanding his relationship patterns. He needs to become aware of what his real needs are and learn new and healthier ways to find happiness in a relationship.

Although people often choose potential partners based upon physical appearance, what most feel is simple body chemistry. However, what feels simple can be quite complex. The basis of attraction may be more than meets the eye and outside your awareness. Think about the factors mentioned earlier as well as the dynamics in the examples of Jennifer and Bob. See if you can begin to identify with some of the patterns in their relationships. Don't give up. Lots of people have had similar experiences.

Like Jennifer, it wasn't just simple attraction. She was repeating old behaviors that were learned. The attractions actually may have been based upon the wrong reasons that were not apparent at the time. The chemistry that you feel in the present may be similar to the chemistry you felt as a child toward a parent. Your partner may have physical or other attributes that remind you of one of your parents. The gender of the parent is not necessarily relevant, as you each have your own personal family history.

The next chapter points out how all these patterns result from childhood experiences, learned behavior, and chemistry. It will explore the role that these factors have played in the case studies, and how old patterns keep couples from getting what they really want and need in relationships. You will begin to recognize repeated patterns in Jennifer's and Bob's lives, and other cases not yet discussed, and then can begin to understand the patterns in your own life as well.

CHAPTER 2

Don't Deny It, Your Past Is Still with You

Lazy summers spent swimming, riding bikes, slurping popsicles, birthday get-togethers with relatives and friends, and holiday wonderlands.

As you get older, you may idealize your childhood. Many of you think you had it great and came from loving supportive families. But if that's so, why do you have so many problems in relationships now?

SHADOWS OF THE PAST

The way you relate and interact in your present relationships stems from the behaviors you learned as a child. Those early family interactions and dynamics played a strong role in creating patterns of behavior that you take with you through adulthood. They will continue to affect you in all of your relationships as adults—including your choice of partners.

You will begin to see how early childhood interactions played a role once you began separating from your family. This is usually about the time you started school. Some of these interactions may be seen in your relationships with your teachers. Think back. Can you remember any patterns you had with your male and female teachers? Did you behave differently toward each? Do you remember wanting to please? Or maybe, you were disruptive in class? These behaviors, whether positive or negative, can be a way of getting attention. Sometimes just a small amount of attention is enough, especially when you only received a small amount of attention at home. You may transfer and act out behaviors that you displayed with your parents onto your teachers, either male or female depending on the parent that could least meet your needs. This may have been a continuing pattern throughout grade school and even beyond to high school. If so, it is important to recognize those established patterns that are probably causing you problems as an adult.

PATTERNS THAT KEEP YOU STUCK

Many of you are now working. Think about any problems that you may have at work. Some of these problems may concern your peers, supervisors, or managers. You may also have had similar problems at other jobs. If so, are you able to recognize your patterns of behavior? Do your interactions with others seem familiar? It's possible that your parents interacted with you in a similar manner. They may have hurt you, made you angry, feel inadequate. However, as a child, you could not defend yourself. As a result, you may find that you have had self-defeating behaviors in several of your jobs. But maybe, these behaviors were learned as a child, and you are still protecting yourself. It is important to be aware of repetitive patterns that may be working against you. You can begin by trying to recognize these patterns. Identify how these same patterns have affected your life in your love relationships. Having this awareness can help you begin to empower yourself in which you become healthier and more productive.

ANDREA

Andrea, age 42, remembers back to grade school. Her need to emotionally connect with her teachers was stronger than that of making friends with her peers. With her female teachers, she tried to be the best student, get the best grades, and was always looking to be helpful. However, it appeared that with her male teachers, she was disruptive in class, received poor grades, and was not a good student. The irony was that with both sexes she was looking for love and attention but in different ways. Andrea displayed this same behavior with her parents. She always tried to please her mother. Since her mother never appreciated Andrea's efforts to be good and helpful, getting those needs for love and attention always left Andrea feeling hurt and not important. Since it didn't happen at home, she displaced those feelings and behaviors onto her female teachers. Andrea also found a way to have an affect on her father. She would behave in ways that would make him angry. But this was okay, for at least she felt noticed. This also played itself out in school with her male teachers.

When Andrea began to work, she displayed similar behaviors to get her needs met by her supervisors and managers. However, in a work environment with a responsible position, it wasn't going to work. Andrea had a difficult time with women in positions of power. As with her mother, she tried to please these women. However, she did not feel appreciated or effective in her efforts. Feeling hurt, Andrea was hostile, had angry outbursts, and became insubordinate. As a result of her self-defeating and childlike behaviors, she lost several jobs.

Andrea has also been unsuccessful in her love relationships. She is not emotionally self-sufficient and unable to love herself. She has been looking for love and affection externally to make her feel whole. She feels so empty herself, that she has very little to give to someone else. Some of her partners felt she was too insecure, selfish, and not giving enough to them or the relationship. Andrea is a clear example of a woman who has been driven by early childhood deprivation. As a result, she could not recognize her own behaviors as being destructive. She blamed her unhappiness on everyone else.

UNDERSTANDING FAMILY DYNAMICS

The following is a short quiz to look back and try to understand your own dynamics resulting from early family interactions—try to be objective. Maybe your home wasn't as ideal as you once thought. When you examine your family interactions, you may realize that something wasn't right or that something was missing. If you feel that with one parent the answer is "yes" and the other "no," then score it as a no. The following quiz may help clarify what your family interactions truly were like during your childhood.

Answer Yes or No to the following statements:

My parents were close to each other.
  Yes   No

My parents interacted a lot with each other.
  Yes   No

My parents' interactions were mostly positive.
  Yes   No

My parents were outwardly demonstrative in their affection toward each other.
    Yes   No

I had a good relationship with my mother.
    Yes   No

I had a good relationship with my father.
    Yes   No

My parents were warm and caring toward me.
    Yes   No

My parents were emotionally demonstrative toward me.
    Yes   No

I received individual attention with guidance and direction from my parents.
    Yes   No

My parents made me feel unique and special.
    Yes   No

My parents taught me how to be a whole, separate individual.
    Yes   No

I felt that my parents understood me.
    Yes   No

If you answered "No" to more than three of the above statements, you may not have gotten what you needed as a child. Some of the statements involve your parents' interaction with you. Even if one parent met your needs and the other did not, the results can indicate that you may not be getting your needs met in your present relationship.

Earlier unmet needs quite likely are affecting your adult relationships. You may try to fulfill these needs with people who, on some level, represent your parents. When this happens, you may find yourself in another dead-end relationship. Through understanding your family dynamics, you have a much better chance of understanding yourself and avoiding or letting go of people with similar dynamics. You may even find yourself in a relationship that meets your needs.

Family dynamics are extremely important. They form the core of all relationships, especially when choosing partners as an adult. Some people have never really understood or worked through old issues. They are stuck in the past. Then they become stuck and confused in their present relationships. It is essential that you learn from this chapter so you are able to let go of the past and begin to choose healthier partners.

You probably have heard the phrases that "women marry their fathers" and "men marry their mothers." That may be true in some cases, however the real issue is not gender. If you are repetitively making the wrong choices in partners, most likely you are choosing people who have similarities to the parent that was unavailable and unable to meet your needs. The gender is not important. A woman may choose a man who is like her mother and a man may choose a woman who is like his father. As you become healthier, you may notice a change in the type of person you choose. He or she may now be more similar to the other parent.

The most important thing to remember is that if you are in a good relationship, you will be involved with someone who has similar qualities to the healthier parent who was more available to you—the parent who could meet your needs. Think back to the relationships you have had. Can you begin to see a pattern?

Many of you may have answered "Yes" to most of the statements in the above quiz. That may be accurate. However, your need to see your parents in a healthy way may be a defense against seeing them for who they were and how they related to you. Children use the defense known as denial in which they are not consciously able to give an accurate picture. In the statement relating to your parents being physically affectionate, many of you may believe they were. But were your parents really emotionally demonstrative toward you, or did you just receive verbal responses like "You know that we love you?"

When growing up, unless there is overt abuse, it is common to see your family as "normal" and like most other families. You thought your family was normal and it formed your world view. You felt that your family was no different from any other family.

DENIAL CLOUDS THE TRUE PICTURE

As a child, it would have been difficult to recognize any of the unhealthy dynamics or interactions that played a large role in your family. If the family situation was unhealthy, using denial may have helped you cope. This denial may persist throughout your adult life. Since it is a coping mechanism, it was useful at the time; but for most, it is difficult to stay in denial through adulthood. It manifests into anxiety or depression for adults. It will also interfere with most important areas of your life, such as your pattern of interactions in relationships.

What occurs is that you recreate old behaviors in present relationships. These behaviors were learned as children by observation and being an active part in the family dynamics. You watched your parents interact with each other. If you had siblings, you saw how they related to your parents and the other children in your family. You were also probably aware of the interactions between yourself and your siblings. However, you may not remember it all or have a realistic picture.

Let's go back and look at Jennifer's case. She easily picks out emotionally unavailable men who fear intimacy and commitment. Jennifer was the middle child of three children. Her family was middle-class in which both parents worked outside the home throughout most of her childhood. Jennifer's family appeared to be close and loving.

However, a more in-depth look shows this was not true. There was a marked degree of emotional deprivation and an absence of closeness. Jennifer did not get the love and support needed from her parents. Even though she made continual attempts to feel loved, she was unable to change her parents to be more loving.

Jennifer's parents had a tense relationship. They were distant. They didn't argue a lot, but it was clear that they were not close. She rarely saw her parents be outwardly affectionate toward each other. Jennifer's father, a CPA, worked a great deal. When at home, he kept to himself and rarely interacted with his children. Jennifer loved her father and made efforts to feel closer to him. He never pushed her away when she wanted to talk or hug, but he never initiated or made gestures toward her. Jennifer's mother appeared to be warm and loving, however, she too was never emotionally demonstrative. She felt overwhelmed by her responsibilities as a wife, mother, and working woman. At times, Jennifer made efforts with her mother as well. Her mother would listen and say she loved her, but Jennifer never felt it. Since Jennifer was in a state of denial about this lack of caring, as an adult she used this denial to view her parents as being more loving than they were.

Jennifer feels she has failed in her adult relationships with men. All she knows is rejection and loss, but she keeps trying and repeating the same pattern. What Jennifer doesn't recognize is that there are chemical, physical, and emotional signals that she's picking someone who's unavailable when the attraction initially begins.

THE "FIXER"

Although Bob's relationships are different than Jennifer's, it's easy to see how his patterns have become established and repetitive. He chooses emotionally unstable women whom he tries to "fix." He thinks loving them will make them healthier and less afraid of intimacy.

Bob grew up in a middle class family in which both parents worked. He is the younger of two boys. His father was in the military, so his family moved a lot. Bob remembers living in different countries. His most consistent years were in high school, where he was able to remain in the same school until graduation. Bob's mother was a writer. A successful journalist, the family also moved for her job. Bob was not close to his father, and he was aware that his father drank too much. As he got older, he realized his father was an alcoholic. His father died at a fairly young age from liver disease.

Bob idealized his mother. He felt close to her. However, she was a woman who couldn't be close emotionally and wasn't demonstrative. She gave her children a great deal of guidance and direction and had high expectations for them. She was narcissistic and did what she needed to do for her and not necessarily what was in her sons' best interests. They learned from their mother that achievement makes you successful and the boys achieved in their professional lives. The eldest became a college professor and Bob became a brilliant lawyer. However, Bob had an issue with motivation. He wanted to please his mother, yet at the same time he was a lazy, rebellious nonconformist. You could say Bob's behavior is indicative of someone who had strong ambivalent feelings toward his mother. But at the same time, he continually tried to please her.

Bob's need to please his mother was very much like his need to please Diane. When he failed in that relationship, it was like failing to meet his mother's needs. The loss of Diane only brought up the older, unresolved feelings toward his mother, which exacerbated Bob's depression and sense of loss. His need to please Diane related to the same needs he had to please his mother. The dynamics involved in choosing women who were alcoholic or had severe emotional problems appeared to be related to both his parents. Bob, at an unconscious level, wanted to fix his father so he would stop drinking. However, he was unable to help his father and felt guilty when his father died. He also wanted to change his mother's narcissistic behavior to someone who could meet his needs.

Unconsciously, Bob felt like a failure. This behavior got played out in his relationships in which he, again, was not allowed to have needs, and again, placed himself in positions of trying to change others.

What is essential here is to understand that learned behaviors in conjunction with repressed or unconscious wishes play a large part in choosing either healthy or unhealthy relationships.

In some families, in which there was overt dysfunctional behavior, it may be easier to recognize. However, our capacity for denial is great, and there may be a different perspective of the reality of the situation. For example, families in which the child sees or is a part of emotional, verbal, physical, or sexual abuse. These behaviors are also learned and they may lead to patterns of repetition in adult life. An example would be physically abused children who find themselves in a physically abusive adult relationship. Even if that relationship ends, he or she may find that they keep choosing physically abusive partners. On the flip side, a physically abused child may continually find himself or herself in adult relationships in which he or she becomes the abuser. In many of these cases, repercussions of the trauma are seen as well as repetitive patterns in relationships as an adult.

SEXUAL ABUSE

Childhood sexual abuse can be traumatic and lead to difficulty with interpersonal relationships as an adult. It is prevalent in our society. Some incest survivors and victims of sexual abuse are more willing to talk about it, and it is becoming less taboo to discuss this issue. We read about it in the media. Oprah Winfrey has not been afraid to discuss the issue on her television show.

Sometimes when there is ongoing abuse at an early age, especially if the abuser is a member of the immediate family, it is much too painful to accept. When someone cannot remember most of the abuse, it is called repressed memories. In other words, the actual incidents are not available to the person consciously. Repressing these memories was a defense so the child could move on without being emotionally distraught. However, repressed memories will manifest themselves in time and will impair functioning in many areas, especially in the area of relationships.

Many victims act out their abuse in patterns that can destroy themselves or others. Working through destructive patterns can be difficult and may even take a lifetime. For those who don't seek treatment, there may not be a healthy resolution.

BARBARA

Barbara, age 51, was sexually abused by her father. The abuse began in early childhood and continued through her early teens. Barbara has little memory of the abuse. However, as an adult, it has affected most of her relationships with men.

Except for a few dates, Barbara had her first relationship with Eric at age 17. It lasted until she was 25. The relationship was, for the most part, asexual. In the beginning, they were sexually involved, but that slowed down after about a year. They became more like brother and sister. Barbara felt safe and secure with Eric. It appeared that she had no life of her own except for this relationship, in which she found herself to be extremely dependent.

Barbara was quiet and withdrawn. She suffered from anxiety and depression. She also had fears of abandonment and rejection, which is common among incest survivors. Eric was good to her. He was loving and affectionate. However, after about two years he began abusing drugs and alcohol. At that time, as difficult as it was, Barbara knew Eric was not right for her and she needed to move on. But she did not leave him for another six years fearing the world of unknown men and possibly more abuse.

Barbara believed that loving someone meant that there wouldn't be sexual involvement. She held on to her belief that love and sex were separate; if someone loved you, they wouldn't want to have sex with you. She was looking for someone who would truly love her and not want to be sexual. Barbara entered into many relationships, which were short-term, and sexual, but not committed.

She was attracted to emotionally unavailable men. Since these men did not love her, sex was tolerable. If she got involved with someone who loved her, she could not tolerate being sexual. It felt unnatural, incestuous. Her anger began to surface. At the time, Barbara was not aware of her patterns. The pressure of being sexual with someone who loved her provoked too many anxieties, and she would leave the relationship.

Barbara continued to suffer from anxiety and depression through-out her adult life. In addition to her relationship issues, she had diffi-culty in work situations. She worked most of her life. But she had difficulty getting along with supervisors and coworkers. She did have close male and female friends and those relationships continued.

Barbara entered into therapy in her early twenties, when she began having panic attacks. She spent many years in therapy working on her problems. Her ability to change her belief that love and sex were separate was a huge step. Barbara continued to improve, and each of her relationships seemed healthier. However, it was not until she was in her mid-forties, that she was able to endure an intimate relation-ship, which included love, sex, and commitment.

Barbara is the youngest of four children. She came from a lower middle-class family. Her father held odd jobs, until he went back to school and became an elementary school teacher. Barbara's mother began to work outside the home when Barbara was 10. At that time, her father had a nervous breakdown. The family could not afford to live without her mother working. Barbara's father suffered from severe anxiety and depression for most of his life. He did not want any children and could be mean to all of them. Any affection he did offer went to Barbara. He was also demanding and dependent, want-ing all of Barbara's mother's attention. Barbara's mother appeared to be warm and loving. However, the reality was that she was an anxious woman overwhelmed by her large family. She was only able to give a little attention, and was unable to show affection to any of her chil-dren. It was as if the children grew up alone. Barbara, in denial, thought her mother was loving, but through her therapy, she recog-nized that both parents were emotionally unavailable. Her mother also "saw the world through rose-colored glasses." She was in denial, so she wouldn't have to cope with any ugliness around her. She didn't see any inappropriate sexual behavior. Her defense of denial also helped her deal with her inability to be a nurturing mother to her four children.

In reviewing Barbara's family history, it's not difficult to see how past emotional neglect and sexual abuse has directly affected her ability to be in a healthy adult relationship. As a result of the family dynamics, Barbara and her three older siblings suffer from emotional problems. Except for Barbara, who sought treatment, none of the other children have been able to sustain healthy, satisfying relationships.

CHEMICAL REACTIONS

Chemistry plays an important part in early development and throughout life. For example, if an infant has an anxious mother, it is common for the infant's chemistry to change, so that the infant will also be anxious or worrisome. You are probably aware that when there are more stressors than usual in your life, you feel different. You may become situationally depressed. Since we know that antidepressants can work, we are able to see that we may have developed a chemical imbalance. Chemicals can be seen working with the fright-flight response to fear when the chemical adrenaline is released.

Research shows that the brain releases a specific chemical when we are strongly attracted to another person. That chemical—Phenylethylamine or PEA—is known as the "love molecule." It is a natural chemical with similar properties of amphetamine. PEA secretion increases in people when they fall in love (Liebowitz, Michael, *The Chemistry of Love*, Little, Brown, 1983).

It is not surprising that this chemical is secreted at the initial stages of a relationship. However, it may be that PEA is also secreted on the basis of attraction to what is emotionally familiar from past-learned experiences. In the case histories thus far, the choosing of partners was not a slow process. The men and women all had immediate attractions to certain personality types.

Each had no problem choosing the wrong partner and ending up busted and broken. Chemical responses played a part in their initial attraction. Attraction and feelings each experienced at the time he or she met someone was a warning signal of betting on a super long shot. We saw four different people with different experiences. However, we also saw similar repetitive patterns. In all cases, Jennifer, Bob, Barbara, and Andrea were not comfortable enough to be themselves because they feared abandonment. In the end, each ended up losing their partner anyway because of not being true to himself or herself.

Barbara unconsciously felt safe choosing those roads. Without therapy and treatment, she never would have made any changes. Her family history left painful scars, which would not heal without help. She had a very disturbed father and a mother who was not there to protect her. It is important to note, that Barbara probably was loved at a very early age, as she did have the capacity to love. Children who are not loved are usually not capable of loving. Barbara now has a loving, healthy relationship.

CHASING FANTASIES

Let's try to understand how Jennifer might find herself repeating these behaviors. Consider her psychosocial history and her family dynamics. Jennifer does not want to be rejected, so she chooses men, who on some level, she knows will leave her. Unconsciously, she sets herself up for that loss. That's what is familiar and is an emotionally tolerable state for her.

This scenario is not much different than the ones played throughout her childhood. The difference is that, in Jennifer's unconscious fantasy, she will be able to change these men and make them love and stay with her. This was something she could never do with her mother or father. They never changed, which left Jennifer, in her adult life, trying to fix and change others. Hers is a symbolic act of fixing and changing her parents. Therefore, Jennifer is trying to do the impossible without understanding her own dynamics.

Many people don't recognize their patterns, until nothing works and they seek therapy. Bob's behavior also shows patterns that stem from behaviors learned in childhood. Trying to please and fix others is also a symbolic way of trying to fix his parents. In trying to fix his parents, he creates scenarios in which he will fail. Why? Because he is creating once more what he didn't get, which always left him with feelings of rejection. His fantasy is that, if he tries hard enough, this time it will work. He can do the impossible. He has to be able to do it in order to undo the losses during earlier times. Bob sets himself up for rejection, as he never felt he deserved to be loved.

Andrea emotionally never left her childhood. She took that child with her through most phases of her life. She was not going to let go emotionally and become an adult, until those childhood needs were met. She was not aware that those needs were not going to be met. Her parents did not meet them. Andrea was not able to work through that pain and rejection in order to grow up and have some of her basic needs met by other adults. Andrea was chasing a fantasy that would never actualize and would only cause her more pain and disappointment.

This chapter summarizes how childhood experiences, learned behaviors, and chemical reactions play an important part in the way you feel and behave. The four case examples illustrate how these earlier experiences have continued from childhood into adulthood. If you see this clearly, it should not be difficult to begin to take a look at your own experiences.

Denial makes it more difficult to trace these feelings and behaviors and begin to work on true intimacy and commitment as described in the next chapter. You can gain the knowledge and understanding needed in order to try to make the changes you want. It can be a beginning toward changing your relationships, changing your life, and finding lasting love.

CHAPTER 3

Fear of Intimacy and Commitment

THE FEAR OF CLOSENESS

Relationships can be very scary. Maybe, some of your relationships didn't work out and caused you a great deal of pain. Whatever the case, many of you truly fear close relationships.

Sure you have good intentions. You want to meet the right person. You want that relationship to last. But what happens when fear rears its ugly head? Two things you may fear most—intimacy and commitment—are often repressed or unconscious, but they can stop you in your tracks.

LOSING YOURSELF

Fear implies danger. No one really wants to be in a dangerous situation, in danger of being hurt. What dangers scare people off in relationships? One is the unconscious fear of losing yourself in the relationship. It's known as engulfment. It's the result of unmet dependency needs in childhood, in which you wanted to be dependent on your parents. You wanted a strong attachment to them. However, your parents were unable to meet those needs. You were left feeling alone and rejected. As an adult, you may find a partner who will allow, and may even encourage, you to be very dependent in an unhealthy way. Losing yourself may also be a learned behavior, observing one of your parents relying on the other for most of his or her needs. That parent became totally dependent and lost himself or herself in the process.

When you lose yourself in a relationship, your sense of identity can disappear, as you turn yourself over to your partner. You can begin to feel unsure of what your identity is after allowing your partner to be in charge. You may become too dependent on your partner, which can have serious consequences.

Fearing intimacy sets the stage for fearing commitment. The ability to commit depends directly upon having a solid sense of self. You need to be your own separate person who can remain separate once committed. It's imperative for you to keep your own identity and not allow your sense of self to be based upon your partner's identity.

FEARS OF ABANDONMENT

You may also fear intimacy and commitment, because you are afraid of being abandoned. As a child, if you experienced traumatic losses either by death of a parent, separation, divorce, emotional, or physical abandonment by one or both parents, you may suffer in your ability to be intimate and commit. Without working through these losses, you may avoid getting too close. You may not understand that the underlying fear is that your partner will leave you.

You may have fears of both dependency and abandonment. What happens if you are too dependent, lose your separateness and then your partner leaves you? You may begin to feel like a helpless child in a great deal of emotional pain—reliving the same pain you felt as a child.

Losing a partner can be quite traumatic—loss of a partner can trigger reexperiencing the loss of people who abandoned you in childhood. If your partner leaves you, feelings of grief can be complicated, as you still have unresolved issues of loss from childhood.

Painful memories that relate to loss become hidden and difficult to access. Instead of understanding the origin of the fear, you may just feel anxious when you get too close. You may also feel angry with your partner—even about something minor—but use that anger to distance yourself. You distance yourself from your partner to feel safe.

You may decide to leave the relationship. Or you may feel that once you have some distance, you can move closer again. For those of you who distance, this may become a pattern of drawing close and then distancing. Sometimes, this is known as the "push-pull" relationship.

As you work toward healthier relationships, having this freedom can allow you to feel less and less afraid, until you are able to commit.

What is important is the extent of the fear, and if it is interfering with your ability to be in the relationship you want. Think about your family history, your past relationships and try to determine if there is a pattern. Think about your goals and how your fears of intimacy and commitment may inhibit achieving those goals.

You are not aware that you have fears of intimacy and commitment. You may have every intention to meet the right person with whom you can have a long-term relationship. However, repressed fears may interfere.

Let's go back to Jennifer, the woman who repetitively chose unavailable men. She had uneasy feelings about some of the things Michael said and did. Although his behavior wasn't perfect, there was nothing that needed confrontation and change. It was more of Jennifer's reactions that told her something wasn't right. She felt this before in past relationships. They were warning signs that the relationship would not be long-term. It was her gut reaction, which was usually on target. Have you ever experienced intuitive, gut-level feelings that tell you something is wrong? These early signs in Jennifer's relationship could have helped her recognize that she was trying to be with someone who was unavailable—someone who had issues with intimacy and commitment.

Like Jennifer, many of you may experience uneasy feelings about things your partner says or does. Some of these may be reactions to overtly hurtful behavior, while others may be on a more intuitive level. You may let all these things pass as if they didn't matter. You may even forget or suppress them. You may also choose to believe that these kinds of negative behaviors will change given more time in the relationship. You put up with these behaviors, because you don't want to be alone. You may rationalize your partner's behaviors thinking your partner will change them and become more available. However, unless your partner shows a desire and some ability to become more committed, you are only reinforcing your fantasies.

EMOTIONAL UNAVAILABILITY

Below are some signs that indicate your partner is unable to be close or to commit.

- Your partner says he or she never wants to get married. Listen—that just might be true. People usually mean what they say!
- Your partner does not want to see you more than once a week.
- Your partner spends every Saturday evening and night with you but always has plans for Sunday that do not include you.
- Your partner begins to call you less frequently.
- Your partner tells you that he or she will have to work longer hours and has less time to see you.
- Your partner's behavior is less consistent in the time you spend together. It feels like he or she is moving away from you.
- Your partner is not as affectionate as in the past.
- Your partner is divorced with children and does not want you to meet them.
- Your partner excludes you from activities with family, friends, or coworkers.
- Your partner's personality and moods change consistently. He or she may have angry outbursts but then be kind and loving.
- Your partner shows more affection to his or her pet than you!

It is imperative to recognize and constantly be aware of signs like those mentioned above. The signs may show up at the beginning of a relationship or later. However, once you begin to notice signs, don't overlook them. Your partner is giving you important information! Don't make excuses for your partner—and more importantly, don't blame yourself for causing the behavior. Blaming yourself only justifies your partner's behavior. Make a decision about whether to continue before you get too attached. Once you are too attached, you may lose perspective making it more difficult for you to act in your own best interest. Don't drag your feet. When you move on, you will be more aware in a shorter time period about any existing problems in your next relationship.

See if you can spot the early warning signs in the following case studies.

JOHN AND MARY

John and Mary have been in a relationship for over a year. John, age 36, has never been married. Mary, age 32, has been divorced for four years. Mary is having concerns about the relationship; specifically, she feels John's is unable to be in a close intimate relationship. John says he is committed to Mary, and believes the relationship is a good one. He feels they are close and says he loves her. However, Mary is frustrated with John's lack of attention.

Mary is outwardly demonstrative in showing affection toward John. He accepts it but does not reciprocate. Mary has asked John to be more affectionate, but John feels he is affectionate and doesn't see any problems. Also, Mary wants to get married, but John thinks living together works great. John doesn't feel a need to marry. He thinks there are too many divorces, and if they are happy living together, they shouldn't ruin it by getting married.

Mary's frustration level is escalating, and they have begun to argue about marriage. She does not want to stay in what she considers to be an uncommitted relationship. To her, marriage is the ultimate commitment. At Mary's request, John agreed to go with her to therapy for professional help.

During the session, it was clear that each had different perspectives of the relationship. John did not see himself as withholding and unaffectionate. He felt he was giving, and that their needs for intimacy were met when they had sex. He did not feel that the outward expression of affection was necessary at other times.

It appeared from this first session that Mary did not seem to have any obvious major issues with relationships. Her first marriage happened because Mary thought it was time to get married. However, she was not really in love. She knew it was a mistake and left the marriage after about two years. Her family history appeared to be stable.

The result of the initial assessment was that John and Mary could benefit from couple's therapy. However, before they did that, it was recommended that John needed to be seen alone. Although, John did not feel he needed therapy, he agreed to come for therapy weekly.

John came from a middle-class family in which he was the oldest of three children. His parents had displayed little affection, and divorced when he was 10 years old.

At first, John reported that he was fine with the divorce. However, after exploring his feelings, he admits to having been frightened. He felt if his father could leave, then maybe his mother would also leave. He began to have separation anxiety when his mother would leave the house, fearing she would not return. John needed her physical presence to feel secure. Since he rarely felt her emotional presence, he didn't seem to need it.

However, it appears that John was not aware of his needs for affection. He learned at a young age that he was not going to get his emotional needs met, and therefore learned to use denial as a way of coping with those unmet needs. As a result, John became more self-sufficient. He put his needs aside to help his mother. He became very helpful around the house. Being the oldest, he felt he had the responsibility to take care of the family.

As result, John had become both physically and emotionally self-sufficient as an adult. He was successful and did not mind being alone. At times, he felt lonely and would enter into a relationship. However, most of his relationships were short-term and never led to marriage.

If you look at John's history, his relationship with Mary would make sense. Mary was a fairly secure woman. Her needs for intimacy were tolerable for John, as she made little demands on him emotionally. It was not until she wanted more from the relationship, and upset the status quo, that John became uncomfortable and anxious.

John's need for feeling in control was great, and his need for intimacy wasn't. Since he never allowed himself to trust and be vulnerable, it wouldn't devastate him if the relationship with Mary ended. He would feel a loss, but not the same kind of loss that Mary would, because she could trust and commit.

After several months in therapy, John began to understand how his childhood experiences played a strong role in his inability to have the kind of relationship he really wanted. He was able to get in touch with his fears and emotional needs. He began to understand his reasons for never marrying. Gradually, he became more affectionate with Mary. He began to feel more secure and was able to trust and allow himself to be vulnerable. He also recognized that his reasons for never marrying were a result of his learned experiences, and he began to feel less threatened about making more of a commitment.

TRUST VS. MISTRUST

Trust is the most important part of a healthy, long-lasting relationship. Many people, like John, feel they can trust; however their behavior indicates otherwise. Question yourself as to whether your ability to trust in a relationship may be an issue. Again, it is important to look at your family history and the issues that may have led to your mistrust. It is crucial to understand how you developed this fear.

Trust requires the ability to be vulnerable with someone else. Feeling vulnerable can be scary. It means taking a big risk. If you allow yourself to open up to another person, how can you be sure it is safe? What if your partner sees the real you and your weaknesses? How can you guarantee he or she won't leave or abandon you? Trust problems can be related to fears of abandonment and rejection. To trust in the fullest sense, you open yourself up to the possibility of being left, as there are no guarantees another person will stay with you.

Just because you may fear abandonment, trusting your partner doesn't mean you will be abandoned. Trust must be looked at as it relates to feeling abandoned, so you can begin to recognize old issues that may be getting in the way. And, being left once years ago does not mean it will happen again. See your present relationship for what it is. Don't contaminate it with unresolved issues from the past. Fear of rejection and abandonment are the most common fears for people who avoid relationships.

Trust is something you feel or you don't. It comes from within and takes time to develop. Trusting is usually a result of behaviors that make you feel safe and secure. On the other hand, allowing yourself to be vulnerable is a conscious act, which means you have to take risks. Taking risks may bring up anxiety, discomfort, and fear. However, true intimacy is never achieved without taking risks. Time and behavior will indicate if a good decision was made.

Trust also involves honesty. Trust and vulnerability demand that you and your partner are totally honest. Honesty involves being direct and straightforward in talking about what you think and feel. The ability for both partners to be honest fosters more intimacy.

People vary in their tolerance for being intimate. When we talk about intimacy, it is not just, as many people think, the sexual part of a relationship. It is the ability to be close on many levels such as talking, hugging, kissing, or just experiencing a close feeling with someone else. Intimacy is not just for lovers. Family and friends can be intimate as well.

If you watch people hug, you can see how different people react. You may see people who barely touch when hugging, or you may see two people embraced in a strong connected hug. Think about how people you know hug. Now, think about what they might be like with their partners.

Hugging is an expression of closeness. How many couples do you suspect are able to demonstrate physical closeness only in the bedroom? And, even in that setting, are they hugging and touching in an emotionally loving way, or are they just having sex? Sex is an important part of intimacy, but it is not what constitutes intimacy.

Are you someone who can easily show affection and touch without holding back? Sometimes, observing yourself and others in an act of expressing closeness and affection can predict your own emotional availability.

Like John, many people feel they don't have problems with closeness. It wasn't until John entered into therapy that he became aware of his fears. He recognized his problems. You may begin to realize that your beliefs about your ability to be close are not true. You need to understand why you have difficulty with closeness and how to overcome it.

THE NEED FOR CONTROL

People like to be in control of themselves and their environment and become frightened and threatened if they feel they aren't. Entering into a relationship can bring up control issues. You may feel that you will lose any control or power you had in your life. However, you know control is just an illusion. The reality of life is that you have little control over much of what happens to you. However, the illusion of control is real, and so is the loss of it. Those of you in relationships may not recognize that you have these issues.

On an unconscious level, losing control equates to losing oneself. The fear of not being in control can be so great that some people avoid any long-term relationships. The severity of your problem determines what you need to do to resolve it. For any change, it's essential that you first recognize the problem. The issue of losing control and losing oneself can be a difficult one, in which the information needed to resolve it may not be consciously available to you. That is why professionals can help.

INTERDEPENDENCY

The ability to be dependent in a relationship is also part of being intimate. You may have heard the term "interdependency"—which means two separate people are together and depend upon each other in many areas of their relationship. Interdependency is normal and healthy unless the dependency changes to the degree in which you and your partner begin to fuse.

FUSING

Fusing implies that you and your partner have difficulty remaining separate. You now have difficulty separating from each other. Both of you lose yourself in a fused relationship. Both of you may be easily threatened by any acts made by one of you that show independence and separateness. Both feel the loss of identity as a separate person and become mutually dependent in an unhealthy way.

Many people stay distant in a relationship or avoid intimate relationships for fear of losing themselves. They feel they are no longer in control over their lives. They recognize they have given too much power to their partner.

Dependency can also bring about resentment. Recognizing how much you need your partner can be scary and lead to feelings of anger. You may feel that you want to run away, but you can't as you are too connected. It's almost like a child who is ready to separate from his or her mother. However, the mother has the power either to keep the child dependent or to permit the child to become more autonomous. This is usually based on how the mother feels about herself. Does she need the child to be dependent, or is she willing to let go and encourage autonomy and individuation?

If you relate to the above description, examine the dynamics between you and your partner. Who is encouraging the dependency, and how did you allow yourself to become so dependent? More important, what will happen if you begin to separate? Will your partner discourage you? If so, it probably means that he or she wants to have you connected in an unhealthy way.

This may not be a conscious process. Your partner may have fears of rejection and abandonment. The only way he or she copes with these fears is to keep you dependent, so that you will lose yourself and stay dependent. Most importantly, if this is happening, you have gotten caught up in a fused state. You need to begin to separate. As difficult as it may be, you gradually have to begin to become more separate, self-reliant, and regain your sense of self. It means having a life of your own separate from your partner, as well as a life with your partner that is mutually dependent in a healthy and productive way.

It is important, however, to recognize that if you begin to become more autonomous, it may threaten your partner. When that happens, your partner may not accept a change in the relationship dynamics. This is bound to bring about conflict. The relationship may enter a crisis period. If, as a couple, you are unable to resolve this problem, the relationship may end.

However, it is important for the one who is making the positive changes to choose which is more important to him or her. Is returning to your old ways going to make you happy? Or is the new self that is emerging the part of you that you like? You need to begin to make choices that are best for your own personal growth.

UNRESOLVED FEELINGS OF LOSS AND GRIEF

Recent loss of your partner may also have an effect on your ability to be intimate and committed. When a relationship ends, whether through separation, divorce, or death, it is natural for the person left to want to connect again. When connecting immediately, it is often called a "rebound" relationship. Many times, unresolved feelings can bring up the unconscious emergence of past losses.

If grief has not been dealt with, being in denial and acting impulsively to avoid those painful feelings can lead to unhealthy relationships. It can contaminate the new relationship and end up in another loss. During these times, you are not only feeling the first loss, but now you may add on another loss. When this happens, it is not uncommon for you to become symptomatic, experiencing feelings of depression, and anxiety.

BRIAN AND ROBIN

Let's look at a new case study. Brian, age 41, recently went through a long, bitter divorce. Since he didn't want to be alone, he began dating Robin, age 40. Brian and Robin were very attracted to each other and saw each other daily. However, Brian continually talked about his ex-wife and their divorce.

If she listened and validated his feelings, Robin felt like she could help him work through his problems. Most of what he felt and discussed was his anger at his ex-wife, the attorneys and the finances that were related to a divorce he did not want. Robin felt by being there for Brian, he would get through his feelings, realize how wonderful she was, and want her even more.

On the other hand, Robin felt that Brian was so consumed with his divorce that he would never get beyond it at this time. Robin hoped, by showing she was not like his ex-wife, that he would come closer.

What Robin didn't realize was that Brian still loved his ex-wife. He didn't tell Robin about those feelings, although she listened to him regularly. Sometimes, she felt frustrated, thinking it was too soon for him to be in another relationship. However, she was becoming attached, and felt he was too. She believed this relationship would last.

Brian and Robin dated for about two years. When they were together, everything seemed fine. However, she felt insecure and she didn't know why. What Robin didn't know was that all through their relationship, Brian had been dating other women. Brian never told her, but she could feel something was wrong. He came home late, and at times, would not call her until late in the evening. She was not invited to some of his family and social functions.

Robin felt like he was there when he was with her, but that he also had another life. She began to feel that no matter what she did, Brian would not commit to the relationship. After two years and an ultimatum, Robin ended the relationship.

In this case, Brian was so hurt from his divorce that it was too soon to move on. Yet, he jumped right into another relationship and did not give himself the time to work through his feelings of anger and loss. Brian had been monogamous during his marriage. He was not monogamous while seeing Robin, which was his way of keeping himself distant and safe. He did not want to get too close for fear of being left again. After their relationship ended, Brian got into another relationship and did the same thing. That relationship also ended. It took Brian about five years until he worked through his feelings and was ready to commit. Brian remarried about five years later.

BILL AND SUSAN

Bill, age 39 and Susan, age 33 offer another example. Bill recently lost his wife to an illness, after she had been sick for about a year. Feeling very lonely, Bill immediately became romantically involved with a long time friend, Susan, whom he and his wife had known. The relationship went well for a while. However, Bill also continually talked about his wife. Susan began to feel as if Bill idealized his wife and could see nothing but how wonderful she was.

Susan felt she could not compete with this idealized woman. After about a year, she decided to leave the relationship. Bill cared a great deal for Susan and was upset when she left. As a result, Bill felt another loss. Since, he hadn't fully grieved his wife's death, he now was grieving two losses. Bill became depressed and needed medication and therapy to help him work through his grief.

Fears of intimacy and commitment are very common. People can come up with many reasons to avoid them. But even if you don't avoid relationships, something may be holding you back from being too close. You may not be aware of your fears.

Most fears are born of childhood experiences. You may not be able to see how your family played a role in developing your fears. You may be in denial. If you don't work through these issues of fear, you will continue to be fearful without understanding it, which will later become evident in unsuccessful adult relationships. You will find yourself scared in relationships in which trusting and vulnerability bring out avoidant behavior. You have difficulty trusting, and you do not want to be vulnerable. You fear depending on another person for fear of losing control.

Of course, nobody wants to be rejected. But are you willing to let fear of rejection stop you from becoming intimate with your partner? Or do you want the commitment necessary to build a loving, long-lasting relationship?

If you now believe unresolved childhood issues, such as those discussed in this chapter, are preventing you from being in a healthy relationship, it is a good time to think about change. Once the problems are identified, ask yourself if you are ready to look closer.

When you are ready for change, you can work on the targeted problem areas and begin to improve your thinking and behavior. Chapter 4 will guide you in this process—which starts with understanding how power works in relationships and the steps you can take to best empower yourself.

CHAPTER 4
Undoing the Damage

At this point, you should be able to recognize some of your unhealthy and unproductive patterns. You may want to ask yourself what are my repetitive patterns? Do I understand, and can I identify the changes I want to make? If you answer yes to both questions, you are on your way toward making changes.

You know you want to be different in your relationships. However, in order to have the relationship you want, you now understand you have to make the necessary changes. And change can be difficult. You must first remember that you have the power to change. No one else can do it for you. You may need some help, but ultimately it is up to you.

In order to work toward change, it is important to be certain that you truly want a different kind of relationship. You need to ask yourself if you are still comfortable with your present roles in relationships, which are familiar from your earlier years. If you are, it is essential that you look at those prior issues to effectively bring about changes.

THE BALANCE OF POWER

The ability to recognize your own power and how it may affect your relationship is very important. The power you have comes from within. It is an inner strength that allows you to feel you are in control of your life. In your relationship, it is important that you be able to recognize who has the power or control and whether the balance of power will meet your needs. In looking at your relationship, there may be one partner who dominates. He or she may make all the decisions. Everything needs to be the way they want it. You have little say in most matters, even if the matter is as small as choosing a place to have dinner. Are you content being in a relationship in which you don't make many of the decisions? Do you feel you should have more of a say? If you do want more of a say, but your partner has difficulty letting go of what he or she perceives as control, you need to have the ability to empower yourself. Empowering yourself means, you have dealt with any self-esteem problems you may have, which have inhibited you from feeling that you have any power. You also need to learn to be assertive. Being assertive means you have a voice which will be heard. You are sure of yourself. You are direct and honest in the way you relate.

You may be in a situation that you feel needs change, and you think that you should have been stronger and more independent prior to entering into the relationship. Before you can be in a relationship that works for you, it is important that you feel good about yourself, like yourself, and be able to live your life as a separate person. When you begin feeling better about yourself, you will want to express your concerns to your partner. Changes can be made through negotiation and compromise, which will be discussed later on in the book. It is helpful to be aware that in relationships in which one person has most of the power, we empower ourselves by taking more power and giving away less. Your goal is to have more of a balance. When one person has all the power, there may be a great deal of conflict and resentment. Changing the balance of power will change the dynamics in your relationship, and thus the relationship will change. Remember, the more power you give to someone else, the more they will take despite their being unaware of how much they have been given or how much they are taking.

MARGARET AND DAVID

Margaret, age 51, is an attractive, intelligent, successful woman. She was married for several years in her early twenties. Margaret divorced her husband, as their relationship was immature and asexual. She felt as though she was married to her brother. Margaret entered into a relationship with Kevin while she was still married. This relationship was very sexual but lacked any commitment. They were together several years until Margaret wanted to move on and meet someone with whom she could have a long-term relationship.

Margaret was about 35 when she met David. He seemed like the perfect mate. He was the man she had been looking for her entire adult life. She fell in love with David and wanted to marry him. Margaret's history reveals that she had a very close relationship with her father. She idealized him. He was smart, handsome, caring, and successful. Margaret felt David had those same qualities. She also perceived her father as being very powerful. Margaret allowed David to have the same power in their relationship. At the time, it was fine with Margaret to let David make all the decisions, not unlike her father. She was also afraid to assert herself with David. Margaret was the little girl involved with her daddy. Margaret's' relationship with David lasted about four months, when David broke it off and began seeing a woman about 20 years younger than him.

As a result of the relationship with David ending, Margaret was devastated for a long period of time. She felt she could have done things differently, and maybe they would still be together. Margaret regrets she let David have too much power and that she was not very assertive. The irony here is that Margaret professionally was very assertive, had power, and was well respected. For about six months, most of Margaret's energy went into thinking about David. As a result, the rest of her life suffered. She was depressed and thinking obsessively a great deal of time about how to get David back. This negative energy affected her work and other relationships.

Margaret has not been in a relationship she truly wanted since her relationship with David. David's rejection apparently triggered familiar feelings of loss related to her father, which made coping very difficult. Margaret dated, however, it was always very short-term. She felt she had to date as a result of peer and family pressures. Margaret, at this point in time, made the decision not to pursue a relationship.

Margaret feels that she is satisfied with her life without a partner and is no longer making active attempts to meet someone. Several years ago, she felt she would never meet the right man. Seemingly, her relationship with David was the only one she ever really wanted. Because the relationship with David was so similar to her relationship with her father, she was setting herself up for failure in terms of meeting that "perfect" man. On an unconscious level, Margaret may have avoided any new relationships for fear of abandonment and rejection. For some time, Margaret was ambivalent about being in a relationship, and her ambivalence was obvious with the men she dated. As a result of this ambivalence, she was not able to form an attachment with someone. More recently, Margaret has become more comfortable with herself and her life. She feels that she is fine alone. She may be doing well, but has she rationalized away her needs to have a partner out of fear?

As previous mentioned, Margaret does have a sense of feeling empowered. Additionally, she is assertive and makes wise decisions. She fully utilizes her empowerment in business and other areas in which she feels secure. However, when finding herself in a relationship with someone like David, she regresses back to the helpless child who feels she has no say. She has lost part of herself; the adult part of her who makes decisions and feels in control. As the child, she is the little girl who doesn't want to make the decisions. She wants to have someone take care of her.

CONFUSION AND AMBIVALENCE

In moving toward making changes for a better relationship, it is again important to determine whether you really want a better relationship. You may feel ambivalent and may not have an answer. You may want to ask yourself the following questions: Will having a partner and participating in a relationship really meet my needs? Am I satisfied with no relationship in my life? If you answered yes to the first question, then you must identify what your needs are and how you would like your partner to meet them. If you answered no to the first question, and yes to the second question, it is important to recognize if having no relationship is truly what you want. You may want to consider whether you have an unconscious defense against more pain, loss, disappointment, and a sense of failure. If you answered no to the second question, you need to begin taking steps to find a good relationship.

Are you willing to make the necessary changes to make a relationship work? If so, will making these changes bring you happiness?

In Margaret's case, I believe she has drifted to the stage where she can be satisfied without a partner. However, it seems she has defended herself against any more pain. There is no right or wrong here. However, it is important to look at yourself and decide what is best for you and is this what you want. Many people live alone. They are self-sufficient. They have a good relationship with themselves. They keep busy with work, family, friends, activities, and their lives feel full.

Again, the importance of the aforementioned is to have you take a good look at yourself to decide whether or not you want to expend the energy in meeting someone and having that relationship be successful. If you are ambivalent, it will show. You cannot truly commit to something with ambivalence. Some people may need to work through ambivalent feelings prior to making changes in their lives. You work this ambivalence through by weighing the pros and cons of change until you feel comfortable. Some people may want/need professional help. And if you are serious about wanting to be in a good relationship, it's worth investing the time to work through any problems that you may have.

The aforementioned material may have given you some awareness and helped you to recognize and understand your own patterns in relationships. With this awareness, you are able to make better choices. You need the awareness of these patterns in order to move on to being open to new and different partners. It is imperative to identify patterns, to own them and to take responsibility for them.

The above is not easy, particularly if you have a history of repeating the same pattern. Are you able to identify how you developed this pattern? You may want to look back at your family history and try to identify some of your experiences that have led you here. Try and recognize whether there are any unresolved issues with your mother or father, which may be playing themselves out in these patterns.

Some common patterns may include:

- your parents' inability to have loved and understood you,
- their inability to have been emotionally demonstrative in showing their affection,
- their inability to have made you feel safe and secure,
- their inability to have taken an interest in who you were, or
- perhaps they were too involved with themselves. You may choose the support of siblings or close friends to help you recognize your patterns and how they developed. Your siblings may be able to identify with the same patterns, which will help confirm how and why these patterns developed.

LEARNED BELIEFS/OLD HABITS

You all grew up with learned beliefs from your families of origin. These beliefs can be social, psychological, and religious. You also may be aware of how cultural beliefs have affected you. Out of our beliefs, we develop assumptions. Since they are assumptions, they may or may not be true. However, as a child, you believe them, because your parents told you these beliefs and assumptions are true. You take these with you through adulthood. You also communicate with your partner based on the beliefs and assumptions that you learned and experienced. If a child observes hostile behavior between father and mother, the child may develop the belief that this is acceptable behavior. And, as an adult, you may believe it's appropriate to act the same way toward your partner. Your partner may quickly challenge your belief, and in order to keep your relationship, you may have to change your behavior.

As a child, you were part of a certain religious community. However, growing into adulthood, you began to recognize that you want to be part of something different than you were taught. You may have wanted to join a new church or temple. External forces, whether they be family, friends, cultural, or religious forces may make it difficult for you to break away. The first part of making any change is to challenge the beliefs you have about moving on to something new. This means change, which as previously mentioned, can be very uncomfortable. You may begin to feel guilty. Feelings of guilt can be very powerful. Guilt can inhibit you from any further movement away from the old and toward the new. It is important to be true to yourself and begin to try to implement these changes. You may need some help in doing so. Perhaps your partner has challenged some of your beliefs. Changing them for your partner will only lead to resentment. In making other life changes, it is important that it must be something you want to do for yourself separate from your partner. If the change you want to make coincides with your partner's beliefs than that is great. But it is important to recognize the difference and move on.

TOM

Tom, age 48, grew up in a family in which his parents had a volatile relationship. His parents were always fighting, however, there was no actual physical violence. His parents treated their two children, Tom and his older brother, fairly well. Tom's mother only showed her temper when arguing with his father. Otherwise, she was a good mother, except for the fact that she had difficulty expressing warm emotions. Tom's father was a caring father. However, he did not hesitate to express his negative feelings about women. Because of his father's resentment of women, Tom began to believe that women could not be trusted, they were dishonest, and they were very selfish.

When Tom was older he held on to the beliefs he learned from his father taught him. He was ambivalent about dating. But Tom did not want to be alone, so he began dating. He realized that women did not seem to be so terrible and selfish. He met a lot of nice women and felt he could have a long-term relationship. Ironically, Tom began to notice that after two or three dates with someone, he would find something wrong with them and then he would stop calling. What Tom found wrong with the women he dated was extremely superficial; these women were too tall, too short, too heavy, too thin, had funny ears, had the wrong color hair, had a blemish on their face. Tom could not get beyond the superficial appearances.

Tom's behavior was like this until his early forties. At that time, he felt lonely and began to try and recognize why he never married and why he couldn't sustain a relationship. He rationalized his questioning by telling himself he just never met the right woman. Tom did this until he began to recognize some of his experiences as a child. He became aware that his mother was not warm and affectionate. He realized that his father's negative feelings about women really did have an influence on his own beliefs. Tom realized that if he got to know any woman well, she might turn out to be mean, dishonest, and selfish just as his father said. At some point, after meeting some nice women, Tom began to challenge his beliefs about women. Tom began to change his thinking about women and, as a result, began to develop longer relationships. Tom was still unaware of how his mother's lack of affection and his parents' constant arguments also played a role in his patterns. But Tom began to accept that if he wanted to keep moving forward, he would need some professional help.

SELF-HATRED

There are some of you who will gain a lot from reading this book. However, there are those of you who feel you are having a more difficult time. If you feel that you are having problems, you may want to consider therapy to help you reach your goals. Children who were emotionally deprived and given a lot of negative reinforcement would naturally have a more difficult time. These children grow up with the belief they are worthless and develop a self-hatred. They do not like themselves and have poor self-esteem. These thoughts and feelings are learned from early childhood. These thoughts and feelings perpetuate into adulthood, wherein you begin to feel you don't deserve to be happy. Your thinking tends to be negative. You may suffer then from depression and anxiety. Sometimes people are not aware of their lack of self-esteem. However, this lack of self-esteem plays out in their behavior.

CRITICAL PARENTS

You begin to think back and wonder, what are other contributing factors that have led to these negative feelings about yourself. Children grow up thinking their family is the "norm." All families are alike. They usually don't realize that this is not true until they become adults. And even then, many have suppressed the reality of what growing up was about. It is important how your parents viewed you; how they expressed those views and the impact they had in your adult life. Many of you grew up with parents who were critical. You never received praise for accomplishments even minor ones. Did you feel special? Self-esteem is something that develops from taking in from your parents all the "good stuff." They made you feel special with a lot of praise. They gave you direction, so you could achieve your goals no matter how small. Maybe you had a dream of becoming specialized in an area in which you had talent. Did your parents encourage this talent, or did they ignore it thinking it was childish? Did they listen to the input from your teachers, or did they just look at the negative and tell you to do better?

Growing up in an environment that lacks love, nurturing, guidance, and praise will show up in later life with self-hatred, low self-esteem, and also have an impact on interpersonal relationships. You may dislike yourself, feel undeserving, and even sabotage anything good that comes your way. Recognition and understanding will allow you to see your past more clearly. You will be able to comprehend the feelings of aloneness and isolation you had as a child. Recognizing and understanding are the beginning of change. It is the beginning of "undoing the damage."

EILEEN

Eileen, age 30, has never married. She is bright, attractive, and while she probably could be more successful, she does have a good job. Eileen dreamed of becoming a musician. Her fear was, as a musician she would never succeed; she would fail. Therefore, Eileen never attempted to become a musician. Eileen's friends often point out her destructive patterns that are derived from her feeling so bad about herself. At times, she feels worthless, useless, and hopeless. However, Eileen has no problems meeting men. If fact, she is almost always in a relationship. When she begins the relationship, she is happy and feels good about herself. She feels especially happy with the love and attention that she is getting.

It is obvious from Eileen's patterns and the way she feels about herself, that as a child, she was deprived of the love that she needed. Because of this, she did not have the love she could internalize, in order to love herself. Obviously, Eileen did not feel loved by her parents. Therefore as an adult she was unable to love herself and others in a healthy way. Eileen was somewhat aware of her self-defeating patterns with men, but she did not know how to change them. She would feel things that went wrong in a relationship were all her fault. Eileen had a very low self-esteem and believed things would never change. Her awareness of a neurotic pattern was limited to observing that she pushed men away. In relationships, when Eileen began to feel close, she would use distancing behaviors. She would become angry, start an argument, and not let go of her anger until she no longer felt threatened by the closeness. Often, she became jealous, accusatory, and made the other person feel like they could never do enough for her. As a result, her relationships would end. Eileen was sabotaging all her relationships. She felt she did not deserve someone to love her. Consequently being close someone became too scary.

Getting close can be very scary. If getting close is scary for you and you are unaware of this fear, it is likely to act in ways that will keep you distant from your partner. In other words, if you are not in touch with your fear of intimacy, you will create ways to avoid intimacy. Patterns like this keep people safe. Patterns like this keep you safe from the fear of loving and being loved, of losing yourself in the relationship, and then being abandoned by your partner. It's safer to push someone away. While you may experience substantial loss, that loss will never be as painful as your allowing yourself to intimately love someone and then experiencing their abandonment.

For many, it is most comfortable to stay with what is familiar. You cannot be left if you weren't in a position to be left. Making changes is just too scary. However, there are people who ultimately recognize these patterns and decide they want to change. Change, of course, is not easy, and in Eileen's case, she will need a lot of help.

Eileen needs to be in therapy to resolve her issues. Her work will be difficult and treatment may take longer than she anticipated. However, if she truly desires change, she will get there. Eileen may still have some issues, but she will have the tools to cope with them. Eileen will find someone with whom she is compatible. It may be that she chooses a totally different type of man than she has in the past. She may choose someone who is perceptive enough to understand, someone who can work with her and not against her. He would probably be a fairly secure man. He would have the insight needed to help her get past some of her negative patterns, so they can work toward a lasting relationship.

You may be wondering if you need professional help. How many years have you had the same patterns? And how severe are these problems? Do you experience depression and anxiety around these behaviors? Some people are able to make changes on their own without help. A great deal has to do with your motivation to change, to be able to identify the changes you want to make and the endurance to be uncomfortable until you have made the change.

Sometimes people change, as they can no longer tolerate the pain they have felt from repeating patterns of choosing the wrong partners. They may have gained enough insight into their destructive patterns. They are able to identify those areas that require change. They may be ready to make a change. Some people make these changes with less difficulty than others. Some have to work harder to actively change their behaviors. They have to have the ability to endure the discomfort. It means doing things and acting in ways that may be foreign. In order to change, you must repeat doing what is good for you even if it is very difficult to tolerate. Each time you act in your best interests, it gets a little easier. At some point, the discomfort is less. When you get to the point where you are reasonably comfortable, you have made the change.

LISA AND JACK

The following case of Lisa will show how it is possible to move toward healthier behavior, which will make for a more satisfying relationship. In Lisa's case, she has been able to make changes without professional help. These changes have come about because she recognized her learned behaviors and experiences from her childhood, which ultimately resulted in her insecurities. She has been able to gain new insight into the transition of insecurities from her childhood into her life as an adult. As an adult, she realizes that in some areas she does feel secure and can function at a high level. It is only in relationships, where her thoughts and feelings bring her back to earlier experiences. Previously, Lisa was not able to recognize that when in a relationship with a man, she would easily regress to earlier thoughts and behavior. Lisa is now learning how to take her healthier parts and to carry them into her relationships.

Lisa made a decision to change some of her behaviors when she began dating Jack. She knows she feels very insecure in relationships. Her past behavior indicates that she has no patience and needs a great deal of reinforcement. She is also aware that she does not express her true feelings. When she feels insecure, which at times is related to feeling angry, she does not express her true feelings. Instead she does the opposite and tries to please. Lisa fears if she gets angry, she will be rejected. She believes if she pleases a man, he will have no reason to end their relationship.

As far as patience goes, Lisa has little tolerance or capacity to wait for anything she wants. She is trying to change this by working on feeling better about herself and by not making Jack so important.

Whenever she is dating someone she really likes, the man becomes more important than some of the more stable things in her life. Lisa tries to move away from this kind of thinking by not always acting on what she feels or thinks.

Jack and Lisa went out one evening. When they parted, Jack said he would call. He didn't say when he would call, which made Lisa feel anxious. At this time in their relationship, Lisa did not initiate any calls. She felt it was too soon to call him. She wanted to allow Jack to come forward and not push him away. Lisa would be making a positive change to follow through by not calling until she felt the relationship was more solid. She felt she didn't know Jack well enough to predict how he might respond. She also thought she might misconstrue Jack's being busy and not able to speak with her. She felt this would make her feel even more insecure. Lisa wanted to do what she thought was right and not act impulsively. In the past, Lisa was impatient and needy which led to impulsive behaviors that undermined her goals.

Lisa expected to hear from Jack the next day. When he didn't call, she felt he didn't care enough. However, Lisa was now able to tell herself not to have expectations, which would set her up for disappointments. She tried using some positive thinking to avoid getting upset, which would usually lead to obsessive negative thoughts. However, when it was almost a week since she spoke to him, Lisa began to feel very insecure and needy. She tried to stop herself from picking up the phone, as this was a change she said she wanted to make. This was very difficult for Lisa, and there were instances where she felt that she was not going to be able to follow through. She was, however, able to wait once she began to change her thinking and put things in perspective.

Lisa was able to recognize that when she felt very needy, it meant that she felt deprived and neglected. She was able to recognize that she was really angry that Jack hadn't called. She also realized if she interchanged the words needy and angry, she would start to feel angry. In fact, Lisa was really angry but had difficulty getting in touch with her anger. Not being in touch with her anger made her feel insecure and needy. Holding on to her feeling angry helped mobilize her to more positive thinking. She was not going to be angry with Jack, as he did not say when he would call. She was using this thinking to help her feel better about herself. Lisa did not call Jack, and Jack did call her within the week. She made a conscious effort not to ask Jack why he didn't call sooner. The relationship was not at that point. Jack still had another life that was very separate. Quite understandably, Jack did not owe Lisa any explanations at this time.

Lisa and Jack dated for about six months. Lisa felt insecure about Jack having too much power in the relationship. She felt she needed to make changes, so she would feel better about herself and the relationship.

Lisa began to take some positive steps. When she did feel legitimately angry, she would express her anger. Lisa also became tired of feeling insecure giving Jack all the power in their relationship. She slowly began to empower herself. She did this by recognizing that her usual behavior did not work for her in past relationships. She felt it was time to take some risks and to commit herself to something new, which would allow her to feel stronger.

Lisa was learning to begin to comfort herself through positive thinking and behavior. She began to do things that made her feel good. In the past, she would feel good only when her partner would do or say something to make her feel good. Rather than ruminate about the relationship, Lisa began to reach out to friends, involve herself in more social and educational activities and enjoy her solitude. By simply pampering herself with a warm sudsy bath, or reading more, she felt good. Lisa was very motivated. She learned to stay in the present and not become impatient with the process of change. Continuing her new behaviors gradually led her to become more comfortable with the changes. Most importantly, Lisa was beginning to feel very different about herself and began to feel more comfortable with Jack. She was able to be true to herself and direct. Her self-esteem greatly improved, and she felt more independent.

Jack and Lisa's relationship slowly developed into a long loving relationship.

It is very important not to place yourself in a position in which you feel there is something wrong with you, and you need to make changes to satisfy your partner. When deciding to make changes, it is important to be aware you are making these changes for yourself. It is of no benefit to make changes for someone who may not be right for you.

"RED FLAGS"

You have probably heard the term "red flags." They are signals you may sense from the other person which tell you something is not right. Red flags may be warning signals telling you this person is not going to be able to meet your needs regardless of how many changes you make. They can be indicative of the other person's inability to be in an intimate, committed relationship.

Red flags can be obvious or subtle. Many times, on your first date, you will hear something that sounds like a red flag. It is critical that you listen to what your date tells you. You want to watch for these, so you don't waste your time in a dead-end relationship—so you can move on to someone who is available for a committed relationship.

Some examples of red flags may include:

She tells you she is separated from her husband planning to divorce soon.

He says he doesn't want to remarry.

He says he will call you the next evening and doesn't.

He tells you about his profession in which he hasn't worked in 10 years.

She talks incessantly about herself and is not interested in hearing about you.

She is not listening when you speak.

He says he is so busy at work that he doesn't know when he can see you again.

She says she doesn't want to hurt you.

He calls at the last minute to see you.

CINDY AND STEVE

Cindy and Steve met on a blind date. Their date to meet for coffee in the afternoon turned into dinner and a long evening. There appeared to be an immediate connection between them. They began speaking on the phone every evening and then after a few dates saw each other every day. Steve began to stay over every night. Cindy was a bit uncomfortable. She felt things were moving too quickly. She asked Steve if they should slow down. His response was that people should see each other all the time to know more quickly whether they are right for each other. Steve did not want to waste time. Apparently, Steve behaved similarly in all his relationships. None of these relationships lasted. Steve had experienced a long painful divorce about 10 years earlier. He was still angry with his wife and would only interact with her on the phone when it concerned their two children. He spoke angrily about her often, but at the same time, stated he had resolved all his issues relating to his divorce. Cindy sensed something wasn't right in the relationship. She even felt the information Steve had given her could be a "red flag." However, she really liked Steve and chose to ignore these feelings. Steve had many other good qualities, and for the most part things between Cindy and Steve were actually good. They seemed compatible on many levels and they really enjoyed their time together.

Cindy began noticing more and more of Steve's insecurities and his mistrust of women. On one occasion, Cindy went to Steve's house for a party. Steve seemed to be distant that evening. When the party ended, Steve wouldn't speak to Cindy except for telling Cindy he was angry she didn't greet him with a kiss when she initially arrived. However Steve chose to hold on to his anger for the entire evening rather than resolving the issue at the time it took place. Once Cindy again felt something was wrong. Steve and Cindy were relaxing by the fire, when Cindy needed to get up to get something and Steve wouldn't let her go. Cindy was annoyed and got up despite Steve's reaction. Steve became distant, withdrew, and did not speak to Cindy until the next morning. It appeared Steve was misconstruing the smallest incidents to make the argument Cindy could not be trusted emotionally. Apparently, Steve was very sensitive to the possibility of rejection. His divorce left him afraid to trust and be committed to a relationship.

Steve would repeatedly ask Cindy about her past relationships. Cindy felt like he continually looked for something to justify his feeling she could not be trusted. She talked to him about how he was constantly assessing her. Cindy began to feel Steve was trying to perceive her as he perceived his former wife; he couldn't trust Cindy emotionally because, she would eventually leave and hurt him.

The relationship lasted four months. Cindy made a cynical remark one evening in front of his friends, which resulted in the demise of the relationship. At the end of the evening, Steve told Cindy the relationship was not working for him. Quite understandably, it was difficult for Cindy to adjust from an intense relationship to no relationship. She was angry with herself. She had seen these "red flags" throughout their relationship. She wanted to believe she and Steve could work these issues through. However, Steve denied he had any issues. He perceived Cindy as having problems, which were intolerable for him.

Apparently, Steve sets himself up in his relationships. He begins his relationships quickly and intensely and ends the relationships quickly. It would appear that on an unconscious level, he wants to prove the relationship will not work. He spends a great deal of time with his partner in a very short period of time. Thus, he feels he has enough information to mistrust the woman and rationalize his need to end the relationship. When Steve begins a relationship, he hopes the woman will be right for him and his children. Steve introduces anyone who seems like a potential mate to his children. His daughter was very excited when she met Cindy and asked Steve if she would be the one. And he thought she might be. However, at some point, Steve begins to get frightened and repeats the same pattern of sabotaging the relationship.

Cindy recognizes she should be more aware of "red flags" or warning signals in future relationships. She would pause and truly hear what the other person was saying and take their actions as an indication of who they truly were. She would believe if someone said something, they meant it and not overlook "red flags."

It is important to recognize your own power in making choices in relationships as well as the power you have in your behavior. You can decide how you want to be and whom you want to be with. With the ability to make choices, correspondingly, you have empowerment and the ability to steer relationships in the direction you wish.

ANNE AND LARRY

Anne began dating Larry. From the first date, there was a strong sense Larry was not someone who wanted a committed relationship. He told Anne he had no desire to ever get married again. Larry stated he simply wanted to have fun and date several women simultaneously. Anne was interested in getting married. Initially Anne thought she had the power to change Larry. Anne was fantasy thinking, which is usually a result of old unresolved issues from your family of origin, which can pull you into a bad relationship. Anne wanted to continue to see Larry. From the moment she met him, she was attracted to him. This was familiar and reminiscent of being attracted to a man who was unable to commit to a relationship. Attraction is often an inexplicable chemical response. For Anne, this response was related to her father, who was emotionally unavailable. Anne's father was physically present, but cold, and distant. She did not have a close relationship with him. She had learned from her patterns to avoid these types of relationships. Anne appreciated Larry's honesty and told him that she would not enter into a sexual relationship with him while he was seeing other women. He said he was okay with that and still wanted to see her. Larry's thinking was Anne would eventually change her mind and have sex with him. It became apparent to Anne, within approximately one month that nothing was changing. Larry meant what he said and continued seeing other women. Anne knew she had the power to make the choice not to see Larry anymore. She also knew, if she continued to see him, she might get pulled back into old familiar repetitious patterns. As attracted as she was to Larry, Anne recognized her empowerment not to repeat patterns and ended the relationship.

Anne was beginning to more easily identify her patterns and became more aware of her choices in relationships. She was capable of using the power of choice to do what was in her best interest and she found herself making different choices in her selection of men. After ending several relationships with unavailable men, she was able to become more attracted to men who didn't fit the old familiar picture. Anne finally found a relationship that was very satisfying. She found an intimate, committed relationship, which evolved into a healthy, loving long-term relationship.

THE QUANDARY OF COMMITMENT

A great deal of men and women have difficulty making a commitment. However, that is not an indication they cannot make a commitment. Timing can be an important factor. Circumstances in their lives can inhibit them from getting too close. However what is most important is to what extent are they truly unavailable and how fearful they are of intimate relationships.

It is important to recognize that you have the power to bring someone closer to you as well as the power to drive him or her away. As in the above noted relationship, it was clear that Larry was not ambivalent. He knew what he wanted and was very clear about it. This was not a man you could bring closer, and the sooner you recognize that in a relationship, the better.

Those of us who have fears of intimacy are usually driven away by those who are insecure, needy, and demanding. Those people who have fears of intimacy need the space to move forward and back until they get to a comfortable place. As their partner, it is to your advantage to allow them the freedom of movement without letting your old needs and fears get in the way. You have to be sufficiently strong and secure with yourself to truly understand how difficult it is for your partner. If you know the other person is sincere in their efforts to change, you can give them the room they need. At times, you may feel they will never be able to commit. Should you experience your partner getting closer and then moving away, it is probably because they are testing you as well as genuinely trying. You need to put your own needs on hold for a while for the other person to feel safe and not threatened by closeness.

JOANIE AND ALLAN

Joanie, age 43, met Allan, age 45 at a singles function. Both Joanie and Allan had been divorced. It appears that Joanie had resolved her issues from the divorce. She had no children. Allan's divorce was a very difficult one, because of hostile feelings, financial disagreements, and child custody issues. Both Allan and Joanie dated quite a bit from the time of their divorces. Neither Allan or Joanie had been involved in a long-term relationship. They began dating soon after they met. Joanie and Allan were very attracted to each other. Their sexual relationship soon began after they first began dating. Joanie felt she was falling in love with Allan. She felt that this was the relationship that she really wanted. Allan was more ambivalent. He knew he wanted to marry again, but at this stage of their relationship, he was not actively committed to Joanie. He avoided talking about the future to Joanie. Joanie judged the relationship by Allan's behavior which was caring and loving.

Joanie and Allan were dating for several months. Joanie happened to notice Allan's appointment book. In reading his appointment book, it was clear from this book, that Allan was seeing at least one other person. Joanie was extremely upset. She didn't know what to do or say. Hence, she did nothing. She did continue to see Allan while he was seeing another woman. She never raised the subject with Allan. While many women would have ended the relationship, Joanie was determined to have Allan as a lifetime partner. Was Joanie being masochistic, or was she taking a risk for something she really wanted? She was able to be strong when with Allan, but when alone and with friends, she questioned her behavior. Several months passed and Joanie did not notice any change in Allan's behavior. She felt Allan continued to be caring but noticed there seemed to be no forward movement in the relationship. Joanie decided to end her relationship with Allan and begin to let go of some of her feelings for Allan. She did not regret her decision. She needed to take this risk and see what would happen. She acknowledged she allowed Allan to have all the power and control within the relationship. She justified these dynamics, because she wanted to be with Allan.

Joanie was healthy and able to hold on to her self-esteem. While she was comfortable to give Allan control in their relationship, she was confident she had the power to make different choices if necessary. She never let Allan know anything was bothering her and she continued to see him on a regular basis, until she made the decision to get out of the relationship.

Joanie and Allan had no contact for six months, when Allan called Joanie and asked if she would see him again. Joanie continued to believe Allan was the person she wanted and agreed to seeing him again. Now, however, any issues they had were brought out into the open and discussed. They were honest and direct with each other.

The relationship was good. They were both satisfied. In fact, they decided to move in together. Living together was sufficient commitment for Joanie at this time. After about a year, Joanie told Allan she wanted to get married. However, Allan said he wasn't ready to marry but wanted to leave things as they were.

Joanie felt she had to make a decision and looked at options. She decided to give Allan an ultimatum, which included a possible date for a wedding. She told Allan if he was not ready to marry her by that date, she would end the relationship. Because Joanie was strong-willed and decisive, Allan took her words seriously. Allan was able to work through his ambivalence regarding marriage. Together, they chose a date to get married. Allan and Joanie have been happily married now for about 13 years. Obviously, they have been through both good and bad periods. The difficult times were usually a result of external stressors. They worked as a team and successfully came through each crisis. When problems arose either individually or with respect to the marriage, they had the motivation and the skills to work through and resolve any issues.

Joanie and Allan's relationship is an example of how you have the power to act in a way that will meet your needs. Obviously, it was difficult for Joanie to continue in her relationship with Allan. However, she was determined, knew what she wanted and was aware of all her options. The relationship differences were difficult for Allan. Certainly, he was uncomfortable being given an ultimatum. However, he too was aware of his choices. Allan made the choice to try to work through any ambivalence he had. He was capable getting through to his ambivalence and moved forward to marry Joanie.

An intimate love relationship involves a long process in which people grow together caring more deeply as time goes on. This involves recognizing that needs change over time and being capable of meeting each other's emotional, physical, and psychological needs. The constant change in needs requires a couple to work through crisis periods. Working through a crisis requires mutual involvement in small tasks, until the crisis is resolved.

A relationship that will endure will result from a strong bond, loyalty, mutual respect, and a healthy independence as well as interdependence. It will involve compatibility on an emotional, physical, and intellectual level.

The message of this chapter is your taking action on changes that you want. You will become more aware if you want to make any changes and whether you are ready to take the risks involved. Staying with what is familiar is much easier and less frightening than moving on toward the unfamiliar, the unknown. Think about the roles that you and your partner play and whether you are content with these roles. Become more aware of the power you have and the choices that are available to you.

Your beliefs will affect how you think about a relationship. You need to ask yourself if you are ready to challenge those beliefs interfering with the success of your relationship. This chapter is about moving forward despite the obstacles, which may be in the way. The message is about committing to change, changes that will enhance you and your relationship.

CHAPTER 5

What Is Love Anyway?

In order to have a long lasting healthy relationship there needs to be love. But what does love really mean?

Freud believed that love is both the foundation of civilization and in opposition to civilization. What about civilization, beginning with ancient civilization? What did the Ancient Greeks and Ancient Romans have to say about love?

The Ancient Greeks, wikipedia tells us, has four distinct words for love. We have but one. The Ancient Greek's four distinct words include: Agape, Eros, Philia, and Storage. The word "agape" in Ancient Greece referred to a general affection to denote feelings for one's children, feelings for a spouse, feelings for a good meal. Agape was used to convey contentment or holding one in high regard. The word "Eros" referred to passionate love, a love with longing and sensual desire. Eros is defined as a love for someone special where that love far exceeds the love of a friendship. The most famous work regarding Eros is Plato's *Symposium*, wherein Socrates' students discuss the very nature of Eros—Impressive. The word "Philia" referred to a virtuous love, love without passion, a concept developed by Aristotle. Philia referred to a general love—between family and friends as well as between lovers. Its definition includes virtue, equality, and familiarity. The word "Storage" referred to affection, a natural affection, one that parents have for their children. Storage was limited to describing family relationships. Interesting that Ancient Greece had separate and distinct definition for each type of love. Perhaps current civilization limits itself by having merely one word, and that may be in part why the definition of love is vague and subjective.

For the Ancient Romans, there again were a few words that correspond to our one love, which were Amare and Diligere. "Amare" was the fundamental word for love. Amare is defined by the Ancient Romans to express both the affectionate sense as well as the sexual or romantic feelings. "Diligere" was defined as affection, or holding one in high esteem and not used in the romantic sense. Again, we note that the Ancient Romans had more than one word to define types of love and current civilization is limited by merely one word.

It is noteworthy that the Ancient Romans' concept of marriage did not necessarily include love. In fact, love was considered somewhat ridiculous and not part of rational thought. Marriages were contractual or arranged and had nothing to do with love. For an Ancient Roman to fall in love with a woman was for him to be taken by her power.

Let's return to what Freud said about love. In addition to Freud's theory of love being the foundation of civilization and in opposition to civilization, Freud had other theories on love. Freud believes the strongest satisfaction is derived from the physical or genital love. Love, Freud says, makes people dependent on the outside world. To love is what brings happiness—not the need to be loved.

Let's now take a look at what Carl Jung, both a student and friend of Freud, had to say about the subject of love. In his 1917 publication *On the Psychology of the Unconscious*, Jung said, "Where love rules, there is no will to power, and where power predominates, love is lacking. The one is the shadow of the other."

Quotation Page.com quotes Jung with the following thoughts on love, "The creation of something new is not accomplished by the intellect but the play instinct acting from inner necessity. The creative mind plays with the objects it loves." Also, he states, "The meeting of two personalities is like the contact of two chemicals' substances: if there is any reaction, both are transformed."

Here again, there appears to be more than one thought, one definition so to speak, attempting to describe love. Certainly Jung concedes whatever love may be, it allows no room for manipulation, dominance, or the need to control, quite to the contrary, in fact. To Jung love is instinctively playful—not from the intellect, but more like a reaction, where both become transformed, a balance of sorts.

And here again, we see a reflection of the Ancient Greeks and Ancient Romans, who did limit the definition of love to one love, one word.

Let's now take a look at what Alfred Adler, a contemporary of Freud had to say on the subject of love. These passages are taken from *Great Ideas from the Great Books*, published in 1963, and Adler's *Philosophical*

Dictionary, published in 1995. It appears Adler, too, reflects the Ancient Greeks and Ancient Romans, in not limiting the definition of love to one word.

> The word that we must examine in thinking about love is "desire." There are two modes of desire, acquisitive and benevolent, desire that leads to getting and desires that leads to giving. The word "love" is misused if it is used for acquisitive desire, and, in that connection, carries the connotation of sexual desire.
>
> Imagine a human world from which gender and sex were totally absent but everything else remained the same. If you say that you cannot imagine such a world, I must respond by saying that you do not understand the meaning of the word "love."
>
> Certainly in such a world, one would love one's country, one would love the friends one admired . . .
>
> The Greeks and Romans had three words for the several kinds of "love" . . .
>
> It is only erotic or amorous love that involves sexual desire and activity, but even erotic love is benevolent in its concern for the enjoyment of sex by the loved one. Sexual activity devoid of benevolent impulse is not love but lust, and lust . . . resembles greed.
>
> Love is always altruistic, not selfish. Only children and childish persons ever misuse the word "love" for selfish desire, saying, "I love candy" or "I love popcorn."
>
> Love is more altruistic than justice. Justice is primarily negative, its precept being not to judge or harm others. But love is entirely positive in its precepts. Aristotle told us that if all human beings were friendly, justice would not be necessary, for if they loved those whom they thought admirable, they would be benevolently disposed toward them.

And again, not only does Adler relate directly to the Ancient Greeks and Ancient Romans, but also he incorporates their philosophies within his very own.

So . . . what is love? It appears love is not simply defined. Perhaps we are placing far too much importance on what love is, as opposed to being capable of loving, and being loved. Love, it appears, is far more complex than a simple word. Love is multidimensional. For certain, we know love is not selfish, but altruistic. Love is benevolent and not acquisitional. Love is to give willingly, without demanding to receive.

And perhaps in the more romantic sense of love, there exists all the loves the Ancient Greeks and Ancient Romans have spoken of . . .

Webster has a number of definitions of love, some of which he does not attribute to an interpersonal love between two adults. Webster defines love as:

A strong affection for another arising out of kinship or personal ties (maternal love for a child)

An attraction based on sexual desire: affection and tenderness felt by lovers

Affection based on admiration benevolence or common interests (love for his old schoolmates)

An assurance of love (give her my love)

Warm attachment, enthusiasm, or devotion (love of the sea)

The object of attachment, devotion, or admiration (baseball was his first love)

A beloved person

Unselfish loyal and benevolent concern for the good of another (the fatherly concern of God for humankind; brotherly love, a person's adoration of God)

A god or personification of love

An amorous episode (love affair)

The sexual embrace (copulation)

A score of zero (as in tennis)

You probably have your own definition of love. There is no right or wrong.

Your definition may be subjective arising out of strong beliefs that you feel make up the meaning of love.

Fourteen men and women were interviewed and asked to define love. Below are the responses received:

"A strong emotional and physical bond that cannot be easily broken."

"A deep feeling inside which is hard to describe. You just know when it's there."

"Love to me is more than trust, honesty, and ultimate companionship. It's a sixth sense of feeling safe, warm, and appreciated. Coupled with that is being attracted to the other person. Sharing all aspects of your life and body with that partner."

"Love is romance, compassion, passion, commitment, honesty, understanding, acceptance, friendship, humor, happiness all rolled into your life together."

"I don't know what love means. I have only had failed relationships."

"Love is something that is planted and grown for all of your life together."

"Love is encouraging growth in one another."

"Love is not material things. It is a matter of the heart. Having felt that I have been loved and been in love with someone before, the absence of that feeling is an empty feeling."

"My definition of love is someone who cares about who you are as a person, not what you do."

"If I knew or suspected I knew about the definition of love, I would be writing the book."

"I don't think there is a definitive meaning for the word love. Love is an emotion that is so fluid and found in so many different situations and different combinations that it's hard to define. But I think that there has to be a physical attraction as well as filling an emotional need for it to exist."

"Love means to me unconditional, that I can truly be myself in the presence of his person, and they with me. Acceptance, mutual respect and kindness, honesty, trust, feeling safe."

"Love is devotion, honesty, connection, and an unselfish concern for another."

"Love is the deep feeling for another's well being. Love is reverence for another's soul."

"Love is connection to another on a deep level."

Most of the above definitions are used to describe interpersonal love. In most cases, when people use the word love they use it in that way. Interpersonal love usually involves an intense feeling of affection, an emotion, or an emotional state.

A number of elements that are often present in interpersonal love have been described well by those people involved in the interview. The definitions were different, however, they all are a part of interpersonal love. Those people who had difficulty defining love also indicated they have not had a lasting love relationship.

UNHEALTHY LOVE

There were those people who could define love but still have been in unhealthy relationships. They are still alone and searching. It's not difficult to define what you would want from a relationship. However, the difficulty is whether or not you are ready for a healthy relationship. You need to go back to the first few chapters, in which finding a partner can be based on unhealthy needs. You may be reenacting old scenarios from your childhood still trying to fix what can't be fixed; choosing partners who will only reinforce those unmet needs.

Love begins by knowing who you are and what you want from a relationship. What kinds of qualities are important to you? Does this person have some of those qualities? In many unhealthy relationships, it may just be the chemistry that feels right. However, as discussed earlier, chemistry can sometimes be destructive. It is important to recognize other qualities in that same person that make you feel like you are compatible. If you share many of the qualities you want and stop acting out old emotions, there may be a chance for a relationship. However, too many people who have repetitively bad relationships do not care about the other qualities. They care only about the triggers that give them intense feelings, mostly sexual, that will again lead to repetitious behavior that won't work.

TRANSFERENCE

People may choose others based upon transference, a similarity, to one or the other of their parents. (See chapter 9 for the use of transference in communication patterns.)

John had a crush on a woman who reminded him of his mother's warm smile and the fact that she was also a blonde like his mother, and finally seemed especially friendly. It's that kind of similarity to early family figures that can sweep someone off their feet and frequently leads to blind relationships insofar as after the marriage, people begin to see that what they originally thought is not what is.

Susan had difficulty finding someone, as she was only attracted to men who were strong, take charge, financially secure, and owned a business—just like her father. Susan dated many men, but if they didn't possess all of these qualities, they weren't good enough. She met men who had a few of the qualities like her father, but it wasn't enough. Susan became disillusioned with these men. She found it very difficult to find someone who met her requirements.

As a child, Susan looked up to her father with unrealistic feelings about who he was. Susan thought there was no other man like him. She said she wanted to marry a man just like her dad. She thought her dad was perfect. The irony was that Susan loved her father so much, she couldn't see him for who he really was. Susan's father was a very selfish man who could not love. He did not have the capacity to give Susan the love she really needed. But, he did buy her lots of presents.

When Susan met Stan, she was in heaven. She finally found a man who had the same attributes as her father. She fell in love quickly knowing this was the right person for her. It wasn't long after they married when Susan became disillusioned with Stan. He was not the wonderful man that she met. Stan did not have the ability to meet Susan's needs for a warm, loving man. She was very upset. Stan was not like her wonderful father. But in fact, he was very similar to her father. As a child, Susan was never able to recognize how emotionally inept her father had been. Thus, Susan was not prepared to meet a loving man, as she was still acting on old unhealthy needs. Her need to repeat left her in a marriage that was not satisfying.

FINDING LOVE

Love is comfortable. Finding someone who shares your needs and interests may not give you that intense sexual feeling, but they can make you feel loved; the relationship is easy and comfortable. Most good relationships are comfortable. Sex, initially, is not always the most important thing, especially if it's a trigger for you and leads you down that same repetitive road. Once you really can understand that, you may be on your way to finding the right partner. Remember, we are only talking about unhealthy relationships. People who grew up in healthy families, receiving the love, caring, nurturing, and guidance they needed may be able to have initial intense sexual feelings as well as comfort. They choose the right person, as they are right with themselves.

Those of you who have been successful moving beyond an unhealthy relationship may wonder if you will "fall in love" again. With your newly developed strength and a good sense of self, you are well on your way. Because you are comfortable with yourself, you need not question your ability to find a healthy relationship. And with your newly found freedom, you may not need to be with someone immediately.

There are those of you who want to feel more ready to end a relationship. However, you are anxious and scared. You fear that no one else will ever love you—you won't meet anyone. You begin to feel ambivalent about leaving the relationship. Your ambivalence may hinder your leaving. You are afraid of the unknown and you may begin to make excuses. Leaving a relationship will be more difficult for you.

We now have an idea what some people think love means. Many of you are now asking okay, I think I know what love means, but where do I find it? What are my odds in finding the "right person?"

There are many people out there. Remember, it only takes one person. People can meet in many different ways. You may have friends who have been waiting for you to leave your present relationship. They are excited about fixing you up with someone they know. You might find yourself on many "blind dates." You may also meet someone at a party, an event, or at your workplace. Many people even meet people by coincidence at the most unexpected times. You may be taking a walk, walking your dog, on the train, in a restaurant, or some other place where you are not actively looking. You may even begin online dating, which works for some.

LIVING IN CYBER SPACE

In today's world, many people are looking for Mr. or Ms. "Right" on the Internet. People spend hours and hours trying to connect with someone through various Internet dating services. Some of these online services require you to answer many questions in order to reveal the "real you" to others looking for a match. Most interest comes from viewing a person's picture prior to going any further. People are looking for people who look good. However, many of the pictures are not current. The people may look nothing like their picture. People may lie about their age and the age of their picture. However, when it comes to giving information about themselves, most people try to be accurate. It's interesting to note, that the person's view of himself or herself is their view, which may be very real to them. However, a perceptive individual knowing that person may think that they are talking about someone else.

Online dating may also involve a lot of back and forth e-mails. E-mails can be anything you want them to be. You may even feel you are "falling in love" with someone, as their e-mails indicate they can meet most of your needs. Some people would rather e-mail than meet the person. E-mails can be very intimate, however, you again may feel like you have fallen in love until you actually meet the person. People wonder how the person they meet could be so different from their e-mails. Many people who do not appear to have problems with intimacy, cut you off after the first or second date—this same person writing all these wonderful e-mails! Then there are those who feel cheated if they don't date everyone who looks interesting. They don't want a relationship. They just want to date as many people as they can —another way of avoiding any real attachment with another person. Others have dated a lot and feel they are ready only to find that they are repeating old patterns of running as fast as they can.

That is not to say that people don't find love on the Internet. Many people do; however, most of these people are not struggling with intimacy and commitment issues. Thus, this kind of dating can really work for them.

If you have unresolved issues and unsatisfactory relationships, online dating may only exacerbate your issues. You may find you don't like anyone. Or those who you do like are not emotionally available. Issues may present over and over with each encounter. This may be good, as bad as it may feel. You may experience constant rejection, but that rejection is telling you something is not right. It may be the beginning of understanding why this is so repetitive. You may not find the love you are looking for but you may begin to find yourself.

Meeting someone who can meet your needs means knowing who you are, loving yourself, and knowing that this time you met someone for the right reasons; that you are not acting out of unconscious wishes to fix this person, make them okay, so you can hopefully work out the hurts from your family of origin. Knowing who you really are and having self-love will most likely play a large part in meeting the right partner. The right partner will also possess these qualities and both of you will have the ability to sustain a healthy relationship. That is the initial step on a long road to love. Love and all the qualities described above take time and hard work. This book begins with choosing the right partner, understanding all the concepts in the book and learning the skills that are essential for a loving relationship. It's hard work but you can do it! All it takes is the desire to maintain that love. Life changes and you must go through the tasks and the crises to get to the next stage. This enables you to grow and to have the capacity for a long lasting loving relationship that will endure.

CHAPTER 6

The Personality of Relationship Styles

In the earlier part of this book, the focus was on people who wanted to learn how to change repetitious behaviors—specifically, these people needed to know how to choose the "who," the type of partner who would be a break from their usual repetitious and self-defeating choice. Such individuals needed to realize that their repetitious patterns left them stuck and, in the end, without a relationship.

In this chapter, the focus will be on partners who are again, essentially wrong for each other. But, because of the unusual or idiosyncratic style of the relationship, each of the partners feels that they are in the unrelenting grip of the relationship. It's almost as though the gravitational pull of the style of the relationship is so great that neither person in the relationship can overcome its powerful pull. And this is true even though the relationship has terrible problems.

Interestingly enough, some of these people are not suffering consciously. It's just that they choose partners who apparently meet needs that are familiar to them and therefore, at first, such liaisons feel comfortable. For example, such people may be reenacting old scenarios that have problems that were never resolved, and the attraction to someone who offers some fantasied possibility of resolving the problem can seem almost irresistible. Other people sometimes simply don't question their relationship choices and just accept them. They are seemingly content, or passive, or overly wishful, and don't want to, or feel they can't change. Others, who actually kind of suffer in an impossible situation, are unable to see change, or for any number of reasons still feel that the difficult situation is still worth it even though their basic needs are never met in such a relationship.

It is the idiosyncratic nature of such "relationship styles" that keep people in the grip of the relationship.

RELATIONSHIP STYLE:

"All Men Must Love Me"

This is an example of a woman who is in need of having all men love her. Nothing else matters—not even her husband who knows it. Lydia has this hysterical romantic need to have all men love her. She needs to fall in love all the time with different men despite the fact that she's married. It's not her intent to marry any of them. She just needs the attention and the thrill of it all. She's essentially always in a fantasy-like state of being attractive and swooning about this guy or that guy. And the love that she's always looking for is really time-limited. Her love simply waits for the man to love her and when he does (if he will), then that frequently ends her swoon-scenario until she finds another candidate—a man to fill the same role for her to fall in love again and to be in such a constant swoon of love hoping that her love object will then love her.

Lydia and Tim have been married for 18 years. Both feel that they were happy for the first few years of their marriage. However, Lydia's flirtation with other men was evident from the beginning of the marriage. At first, it seemed to Tim that she was no longer happy with him. However, Lydia reassured Tim that she loved him very much. However, she simultaneously had this great need to have other men be attracted to her. She felt empty with only one man loving her. She needed to be desired by all men! And in order to accomplish this love wish, Lydia would occasionally even act out her need of seeing other men. She did, in fact, love Tim, but it didn't seem to matter anymore, as the need to be loved by other men took over and began to characterize the relationship style of their marriage. She felt very driven to find love at all costs—mostly described as the quest for attracting love from other men so that she could nurture her constant need to be in a swoon. This was fed by her knowledge that some other man was interested in her or loved her.

Now, here is the other part of this "all men must love me" relationship style: Tim was aware that Lydia had this roving eye habit. At first, he thought perhaps she was unfaithful, and began to feel rejected and unloved. However, he gradually began to realize that no matter what

Lydia did, she would not leave him. When this finally dawned on him, he began to rationalize her behavior by thinking something was wrong with her. He knew he wouldn't leave her, as he felt no matter what she did, she really did need him and she really loved him. Actually, they both felt they needed each other. Lydia kept promising that each of these short-term love excursions were really not important and were really not serious. And Tim started to believe her when it occurred to him that Lydia was acting as though he was her father, and that they were both happy that her flirtation was akin to her getting ready to go out on a date. Whenever she had such a flirtation, she would preen and get dressed up and then she and Tim would go to this or that friend's get-together, and there, Lydia would meet the man with whom she had the fantasy of love. Tim realized she couldn't stop herself. However, he knew his choices were limited, so he began to look at these affairs as an adolescent silliness or even illness.

Eventually, Tim felt that Lydia needed help and approached her about it. However, she refused to seek help saying these were nothing but innocent dalliances. However the reality was that such "dalliances" meant everything to her. Lydia was so wrapped up in her swooning-need behavior that she didn't even worry about the possibility of Tim leaving her. And this behavior continued for many years with both Lydia and Tim accepting that this was a part of their relationship, their marriage. Of course they would stay together because they loved each other, but Lydia would continue to scan her environment for fantasy lovers, and Tim would continue to fill the role as her husband/father to Lydia's role as the love-hungry wife/daughter.

Lydia's underlying problem was with her father. Her complaint was that her father never gave her the love and attention she needed. In addition, her mother was immature and demanded her way all the time. Lydia became, it seemed, a perfect fusion of being immature like her mother and constantly seeking the attention of her father, and all of it in one person—herself.

Tim grew up in a family in which "children were seen but never heard." He grew up with an overbearing mother and a complacent father who endured his wife's behavior of always getting her own way.

As a thumbnail sketch, it became relatively easy to see how such a combination of needs in each partner enables this kind of relationship to sustain itself—to weather the stresses of love fantasies on the part of one person, and protective and compliant behavior on the part of the other person.

RELATIONSHIP STYLE:

"I'LL MAKE YOU FEEL MISERABLE, AND THEN I'LL APOLOGIZE"

Jean and Paul had dated for two years. Paul was wonderful and made Jean feel like a princess. He showered her with compliments and gifts. Jean felt she was the luckiest woman alive. Paul felt empowered by the control he had over Jean. After two years, Jean moved in with Paul who wanted to marry her. She was happily overwhelmed and they married. It was at this time that Paul seemed to change. He became angry and critical of Jean. Jean felt that this was temporary, as this was not the man she dated. She began to get more and more confused, as the more time that went by, the nastier and more critical Paul became. Jean's response to his anger was to constantly try to explain herself. She still felt that Paul could do no wrong and began to feel something was wrong with her—that maybe she deserved this kind of treatment.

Paul had actually become emotionally abusive. However, after his bout of rage, he was always apologetic, bringing Jean gifts—just the way he did when they were dating. When Paul would make up to Jean, she was instantly relieved and able to overlook his anger. It felt to her that everything was good again. Of course, that was until the next time in which he repeated the same behavior.

Paul's pattern became repetitious, while Jean still remained in denial.

She kept the dynamics of their relationship to herself—not even sharing these scenarios with her best friend. She wanted people to think that all was fine. Jean wasn't aware that little by little she was losing her self-esteem and felt more and more undeserving. She still tried to justify Paul's behavior thinking he would change; especially when he came home with presents after his bouts of anger and criticism.

Jean did not have a life of her own. She stopped working, as Paul told her it was not necessary for her to work. He felt it was understood that he would take care of her. She began to see family and friends less frequently and always wound up making excuses: she was too busy, she was ill, or, that they had other specific appointments to keep. After a while, Jean did, in fact recognize that she had become a different person. Then, she felt depressed and alone. However, she felt she had no choice but to stay with Paul, which she did.

Paul felt he couldn't help himself. As a child, he had a very critical and angry father who was emotionally abusive to both him and his mother. When Paul became an adult, he began to identify with his father, the aggressor, and of course as is usually the case in such instances, he repeated his father's behaviors.

As a child, Jean came from a family with similar dynamics. Her father was also very angry and emotionally abusive to Jean, her sister, and her mother.

When Jean grew up, she identified with her mother who was passive but remained in the marriage. The "relationship style" here carried the consistent message that Paul was delivering: I'll make you feel miserable and then I'll apologize with a gift. And Jean's response was that she was relieved and finally felt understood by him. It was her gratitude to his conciliation that kept her in the relationship. He was mean and then conciliatory and she was hurt and then grateful.

Thus, she was hurt by his meanness, but grateful for his conciliation. And this constituted their relationship style.

RELATIONSHIP STYLE:

THE BOTTOMLESS PIT OF TROUBLES

Judy met Richard when she finished high school. He was her first relationship. Richard dated several girls, but when he met Judy, he became monogamous. Richard did not finish high school and began hanging around with other high school dropouts. When they first met, Richard was not working. He began to play around with drugs like marijuana. It didn't seem to upset Judy. All she cared about was the way he treated her. And he treated her very well.

Richard became more and more involved with drugs. When he began using heroin, Judy got scared and threatened to leave him. She did, but actually only for a few hours. She felt he needed help, and she was going to help him get off the drug. Richard continued to treat Judy well, however, since he got hooked on heroin, he would take her home at the end of the evening and then begin his own. He went to clubs, met other girls and did not remain monogamous. Judy would hear that he was seen at clubs, but she didn't listen.

Judy was childish in many ways. She was naïve and immature. She spent all her free time with Richard. When around others, it felt as though she was hiding behind him. It soon became obvious that Judy became very dependent on Richard—dependent to the point in which he became her drug of choice.

Even though Judy did not use drugs, she did hang around with the same drug-using crowd as Richard. She was obviously in denial that she was dating someone who not only used drugs but also had emotional problems. She was so enmeshed with Richard that she lost herself. She began college and was an average student, as she had difficulty concentrating. She also began to have problems with depression and anxiety. Richard became her world, and she wanted to marry him. Richard was not as dependent on Judy, but did want to marry her. They agreed to marry in two years, when they would both be 21.

Judy gradually became concerned about Richard and began to encourage him to find work, so they would have some savings when they got married. However, Richard needed to get off heroin as his first priority and he wouldn't. Now Judy was in a fix, and her anxiety became worse as she became more dependent. She knew she couldn't marry Richard, but she let the relationship continue. She, again, thought things would change. And Richard cared a great deal for Judy. In fact, he became dependent on her so that she would be there for him. He loved her and wanted to make her happy.

Richard came from a home in which his father left his mother when he was about five. His father was an alcoholic and a gambler. He only saw his father when visiting the bar where his father worked as a bartender. Richard's mother was depressed and for all intents and purposes, had no life. She became overprotective of Richard, which in turn he found suffocating. However, he always treated his mother well.

Judy's parents were practically emotionally nonexistent. Her father suffered from severe depression. Her mother suffered from anxiety feeling overwhelmed with four children and a sick husband. Judy grew up as if she were alone, had no direction, and desperately wanted to be loved. She was deprived of the kind of caring that makes one a whole, separate person with a good sense of self.

Thus, in this bottomless pit of troubles, each of the partners are bound in a strong need system of searching for relief from tension and insecurity. In the absence of a necessary background of trust in the good judgment of parents, both Judy and Richard were safely ensconced in their little nest of togetherness despite the storm of problems surrounding them and affecting them.

RELATIONSHIP STYLE:

"If You Stay Depressed, I'll Take Care of You"

Carol and David have been married for 25 years. They dated for two years prior to getting married. Both of them seemed very happy. Directly after their wedding, they took a bus to the country for their honeymoon. On the bus, David began to cry. He didn't know why, but he started to feel depressed. Carol was confused and didn't understand this strange behavior—especially on the day of their wedding!

David was depressed and it wasn't short term. Over the years, he had a number of episodes of severe depression. He suffered from moderate depression and anxiety most of his married life. He sought help from a psychiatrist and tried various medications. He kept changing medications, as they did not work to relieve his symptoms.

David and Carol had four children. Carol felt overwhelmed much of the time, as she felt David was like her fifth child. She didn't have much time for the children, as she was always attending to David's needs first. David was so involved in feeling bad, that he had no time for Carol or the children. David was very dependent on Carol and wanted her undivided attention. He would become angry when she paid attention to the children, as his needs were not being met. His main role in the family was to provide for them financially—which he did as a schoolteacher. However, he would get more depressed feeling he was unable to provide adequately. When the children were still young, Carol began to work to help out financially.

Carol became very anxious and angry. However, she did not show it and continued to take care of David. She never complained. It appeared that she was comfortable with his inability to perform as a husband and father. It gave her a sense of control over him. She felt she had no responsibility to him except as a "mother." She was relieved of her responsibility to have a sexual relationship with David. She never really liked sex, and now, it would not become an issue in their marriage. At times, he wanted to be sexual. Carol went along with it to appease him, however, she never felt like his need for sex was that demanding. What David really needed was a "good mother."

Carol never really felt happy being in this marriage. She felt she should have never married. She tolerated the marriage, as she wanted her children. She actually thrived on David's depression to avoid or keep adult interaction limited. Her role as his caretaker gave her enough emotional distance.

As a child, David grew up with a mother who was cold and critical. She treated David as a helpless sick child, after he had some back surgery. She reinforced to him that he was not capable of taking care of himself and would never amount to anything. She never reinforced any of his positive qualities. David grew up feeling worthless and inadequate.

Carol grew up in a family where her father was absent. He treated her mother terribly. He was a womanizer and he was never a real father. He was never home and left her mother when Carol was a teenager. Carol's youngest sister was sexually abused by her father. Carol cannot remember but thinks she may have also been abused. Carol was the oldest and had to quit school and work to help support the family. She learned how to be a caretaker and learned to dislike men.

The "relationship style" that exists between David and Carol appears to be mutual. If David is to cope with his depression, he wants Carol to take care of him. Carol knows while David is depressed, she has no responsibility to be intimate with him. Although Carol is not happy, this is the only way she can survive in this marriage. Since David cannot rid himself from depression, he continues to need the "good mommy," and Carol can provide those needs.

RELATIONSHIP STYLE:

HIDDEN AGENDAS

Kathy and Doug have been married for 20 years. Doug has his own business and Kathy doesn't work. They are financially secure, enough so that Doug could retire. They also have two grown children living in other areas of the country.

Kathy and Doug met in college. They were both excellent students and they both enjoyed dating. They began to date each other, but Doug found he had difficulty dating only one person. He enjoyed the freedom of dating several girls at the same time. Kathy didn't know he was seeing other people while they were dating. After about a year, Doug stopped seeing these other girls. He wanted to marry Kathy. Both of them had dreams of becoming very successful and enjoying all that life had to offer. They wanted children, a huge house, several cars, to take trips and travel. And, off course, they would have to have a full-time nanny for their children.

Doug and Kathy married about a year later. After about six months, Doug began to feel unfulfilled in the marriage, feeling that he needed more sexual freedom. He began to work later at the office to keep busy and to deny his need to be with other women. However, that wasn't going to work for him. He began to see other women, and found himself seeking relationships outside of the marriage.

Kathy suspected that Doug was unfaithful. Initially, she confronted him and he adamantly denied having any affairs. Doug had no intention of leaving Kathy. However, he knew he wasn't going to give up the lifestyle he created. In fact, there was a limited display of affection and their sexual relationship continued sporadically.

Kathy didn't believe Doug. However, she decided that it was not in her best interest to leave the marriage. Doug was beginning to do well in business. Kathy saw a lot of money in her future and wasn't going to give that up. She felt if he was getting his needs met outside the marriage, she would get her needs met but in a different way. Kathy was going to treat herself to all that she desired. She had some wealthy friends. The shopping and lunches began, and Kathy was spending a lot of money. She took trips with her friends and began to fulfill some of her dreams, but not with Doug.

Doug and Kathy's relationship continued in this manner for years. They didn't talk about their relationship. Doug was not upset with Kathy's behavior and he didn't feel guilty about his own. Kathy became indifferent to Doug's infidelity.

Doug's underlying problem was that he never received the love and attention he needed from his father or mother. His father was away a great deal of the time traveling for his job. His mother was passive and not emotionally demonstrative.

Kathy also grew up in a home in which her father worked a great deal of the time. She never really received the attention she needed from him. Her mother was limited in her capacity for nurturing and being available to Kathy and her siblings.

This is a "relationship style" in which both Kathy and Doug have accepted the limitations in their relationship. They both have their own hidden agendas, and they actually feel they can live this way. Neither of them is terribly unhappy, and both are getting some of their needs met.

RELATIONSHIP STYLE:

"Leave Me Alone and You Won't Be Alone"

Ginny and Craig, presently married over 35 years, met when they both finished high school. The dated for about two years and got married. They have two children.

When Ginny and Craig first met, they spent an enormous amount of time together. It was as if neither of them wanted to be home with their families, and they were both running away from something very uncomfortable. They found comfort in their relationship and were happy.

Ginny was a very anxious person who found it easy to be with Craig. She found that her anxiety lessened when with him. Craig was quiet. He seemed stable and a good match for Ginny.

Craig was a lawyer who worked for himself. He didn't like working for or with anyone. He was very comfortable by himself. Ginny was a stay-at-home mom until the children were grown. She continued to stay at home until it became very uncomfortable. She was beginning to feel as though she was living alone. At that time, she took a full-time job in sales.

Over time, Craig became unresponsive and wanted to be left alone. He had no friends and was a loner. You could talk to Craig, but only about concrete issues. He had suppressed most of his emotions. It almost seemed like he had no feelings. However, he liked going to dinner and he liked to travel. He was also a very reliable and responsible man always trying to do the right thing.

The living situation continued to be very uncomfortable for Ginny. She realized early on that she did not have a close relationship with Craig. Ginny always felt this way after they were married. However, she had the children to distract her. Ginny was also able to rationalize Craig's behavior. She didn't want to be alone. She felt unattractive and boring and didn't think another man would find her appealing. She never discussed her feelings about her relationship with anyone. She always went along saying that things were good. Ginny didn't see a way out of this, so she began to accept the present and what would probably be the future. Ginny still suffered from constant anxiety. And she suffered alone.

Ginny grew up with both a very anxious mother and father. She also had a brother who was mentally ill. Ginny always felt alone at home. She did not receive much attention from either parent.

Craig was the oldest of four children in a chaotic family situation. His father who suffered from anxiety and depression was emotionally absent. His mother was physically present, but she was unable to show any emotion. There was no closeness in the family. The main mode of interacting was to argue. This was probably due to the fact that the children were not taught constructive ways to communicate.

"Leave me alone and you won't be alone" sums up the "relationship style" for this couple. Craig needed to be alone having very little interaction with anyone. He did not want Ginny to need him in any emotional way.

Ginny knew that if she required anything emotional, she would be turned away. She didn't want to be alone and start over being single. Ginny accepted the part of the bargain that she was given in order not to be alone.

RELATIONSHIP STYLE:

A FALSE AND STEADY SENSE OF SECURITY

Gloria and Jim have been living together for about 10 years. They are both from South America. They have lived in the United States for over 40 years and are in their late fifties. They met at a mutual friend's house and began a very passionate love affair. Gloria has been working all of her adult life and has saved enough money that she could easily retire. Jim has not worked for years except for odd jobs here and there. Gloria has never been married. Jim was married when he was younger which ended in divorce. There are no children.

For the first few years, Gloria thought that the relationship was going well. However, Jim began showing some irresponsible behavior. He dabbled in drugs paid for by Gloria, although she thought the money was going for other things. He also had affairs that he kept very secret. Gloria was faithful and loving and wanted to be with Jim. She thought he was wonderful. She was able to dismiss any thoughts that she had which would indicate that he was not reliable or responsible. Gloria wanted this relationship and would never leave him. She did not share any doubts she had with friends or family, as she needed to believe that there were no problems. Her use of denial allowed her to remain in the relationship for many years.

Jim began to get more involved in drug use. Gloria became aware and felt he needed treatment. He agreed and went to a facility in a different state to get treatment. Jim stated he was in treatment for about two years coming home about once a month. Gloria paid for his airfare and living expenses while he was away. Unknown to Gloria, Jim never went for treatment. In fact, he began another relationship while away and was living with another woman. Still, he came home to be with Gloria acting like the faithful partner. It seemed that Gloria must have known about his behavior, however, it didn't seem to upset her. She told friends that Jim was in treatment for a long time. Most of her friends confronted her on his behavior, as it just didn't sound right. However, Gloria defended Jim and remained in denial. She was going to be in this relationship at all costs. And, the financial and emotional costs were great.

Recently, Jim came home again to be with Gloria. He told her now that since he has finished his drug rehabilitation, he plans to stay at home, take on some handyman work, and their relationship would return to normal.

Gloria is not sure what Jim will do. There are times she wonders why she stays in the relationship. However, most of the time, in denial, Gloria wants to be with Jim. She is very happy that he is home.

In this scenario, the "relationship style" is one, which involves a false sense of security for Gloria and a steady sense of security for Jim. Gloria doesn't want to be alone, but her behavior indicates that she needs distance. In order to meet her needs, she does not mind that Jim takes advantage of her in any way he can. Jim has all he wants. He gets shelter when he wants it, money when he needs it, and a steady woman in his life who will put up with all his behaviors. This relationship style works for both of them.

Gloria came from a family in which both parents worked full-time. Neither parent provided her needs for closeness. They were both physically and emotionally absent. This may account for Gloria's need to have distance in her relationships with both men and women.

Jim grew up with a father who was not attentive. His father was away a lot "doing his thing" whether working, with friends or drinking. He expected his wife to play a submissive role in the marriage, which she did. It appears that Jim has played out his father's role in his present relationship.

CHAPTER 7
Living Arrangements

People date and they may eventually become committed to each other. They realize at some point in the relationship that it's time to make some decisions about how they want to live their lives as a couple. These decisions may be easy, or they can be a source of conflict. People have different needs. Many people are aware of their needs and know how they want those needs met in their relationship. They know their "comfort zones" and some people are not willing to deviate even for their partner. Although, it seems that most are willing to negotiate to meet the needs of each other and the relationship. This may or may not include marriage—it may or may not include living together.

In the following examples, you can see how couples negotiate and manage their living arrangements. There is no right or wrong in what couples choose to do. It's a matter of what will work for each person.

TOGETHER AND SEPARATE

David and Arlene live together on weekends. They spend the entire week separate and on Friday evening after work Arlene goes directly to David's apartment and stays until Monday morning. The following week they repeat the same pattern, although this time David spends the weekend at Arlene's apartment. They follow this arrangement on a regular basis.

David, age 52, has never been married. At this time, he does not want to be married or to have children. He presently works as a graphic designer crafting book covers for a publisher. He puts in many hours and prefers to be alone when he comes home from work. He is nearly exhausted and has very little energy for anyone else. David was an only child and has learned to spend a great deal of time alone. He is comfortable with himself, his surroundings at home and enjoys having his "downtime" during the workweek.

David began dating more seriously after college. He dated Nancy for about two years. Nancy wanted to spend time with him everyday. He also dated Sarah for about two years. Sarah wanted to get married. David ended both relationships. Initially, he didn't understand his need to end each of his relationships. He remembers feeling that he didn't love either of them enough to make a greater commitment. David later realized that he felt angry at some point in each of those relationships. Out of his anger, he would start to feel indifferent towards each of these women. These feelings emerged usually around the time the woman wanted to spend more time with him or wanted to get married. David remembers feeling like he was being smothered and trapped in a place he didn't want to be. These experiences led him to recognize his need for "space," to be alone a good deal of the time.

Arlene is a 50-year-old divorced woman. She was married to Ted for seven years. Arlene didn't want the responsibility of being a mother, so they didn't have any children. Arlene also felt smothered in her relationship with Ted. Prior to marrying Ted; she dated a lot but only had short-term relationships. Arlene felt she probably had a problem committing, and therefore, ended those relationships. However, she was able to recognize, that it wasn't a fear of commitment but a fear of feeling suffocated by those men.

When she met Ted, it was easy. He made no demands, had his own life and gave her a lot of space. The relationship went smoothly for a few years until Ted demanded more of Arlene's time. He then wanted to be with her all the time when he was not at work. Arlene began to get angry and Ted could not understand her need for so much time alone. There was no change even though Arlene made her needs very clear. Conflicts began and the marriage ended.

Arlene works as a copy editor and has her own small public relations firm. She works a great deal of the time and treasures her "downtime" in the evenings. She has several close friends and is presently living part-time with David. David and Arlene have been together for 15 years. They met at a book fair, where her public relations firm was hired to publicize the book fair. David was hired by Arlene on a moonlighting basis to do the graphics for the publicity.

Arlene found herself attracted to David and invited him to have a drink with her at the end of the day. It seemed that the attraction was mutual. They went for a drink, which led to their dating. There were no demands placed by either of them and the relationship felt comfortable and easy. They agreed to see each other only on weekends having a mutual respect for each other's need for space. They did speak on the phone several times a week.

After about six months, Arlene and David agreed to live together part-time. Both felt a little uneasy, but had strong feelings about taking this step. They did discuss the arrangement prior to doing it, and each was clear as to what they needed. This arrangement was working well for them. Their living arrangement fit them based upon their needs for short-circuiting frustrations that arise from too much contact. They needed less contact to avoid what would have been dangerous for the relationship.

Arlene and David felt lucky to have found one another, as each of them finally felt understood by their partner. When they would meet Friday after work, it was their tradition to have a quiet dinner out at a softly lit, romantic restaurant with nice ambience listening to soft jazz. These kinds of traditions they set up in the relationship kept them in a very good "getting-along" state, and the relationship in this particular living arrangement became permanent and exists to this day. David states that "we can't wait to see each other by the time Friday night rolls around, and we look forward to Monday morning when we can be alone again."

"WE'RE NOT MARRIED, WE JUST LIVE TOGETHER"

Charles and Karen have a living arrangement in which they are not married but live together full-time. They both have had arrangements with other people that had not worked for them. Each has finally found the arrangement that works for them. They have been living together for five years.

Charles is 39 years old. He has been married once and is now divorced. He has one child, Brian, who is seven years old. Both he and his ex-wife have joint custody of their son. Their arrangement is working well. Charles has Brian every other weekend and sees him Tuesday and Thursday evenings. He takes Brian to school after the weekend and weekday visits. Brian is adjusting well. He enjoys being with his father and gets along great with Karen. He feels like he has four parents. His mother remarried five years ago. She has a good relationship with her husband and Charles.

Charles has one brother. He was fourteen and his brother was eleven when their parents divorced. Both went through a long period of fear, anger, and confusion. The adjustment to the change in their family was very difficult for both of them.

Charles is a dentist. He works long hours and has little free time. Both Charles and Karen share the responsibility of taking care of Brian when he stays with them. Initially, Charles was very shy when it came to dating. He dated regularly but kept his relationships short, being fearful of getting involved. His fear manifested in always finding something wrong with the woman he was dating, so he could get "turned off" and break off the relationship. Charles wanted a long-term relationship, but it seemed that he sabotaged the possibility of these relationships and always ended up alone and lonely. Charles was not consciously aware of this behavior. Ultimately, when Charles was 34, he met Karen.

Karen is a 40-year-old woman who is also divorced with no children. Karen was married for five years to Peter. The first two years were good and then the marriage began to go downhill. They argued a lot, both had trust issues, and there was little intimacy.

Karen was the oldest of three children. Her parents divorced when she was about 13 years old and she did not take it well. She didn't understand why they had to divorce and she tried as much as she could to talk them out of separation. Her father left the house and Karen was devastated. Since Karen was the oldest, her mother began to give her more responsibility with the other children. She was very unhappy. She just wanted her parents to stay together.

Presently, Karen works as a high school counselor. She loves her job and working with students of this age. She feels she is helping these children especially the children whose parents are in the process of divorce.

Karen and Charles met through a mutual friend who felt they would have a lot in common. They went to dinner for their first date and were both cautious but were able to enjoy good conversation. They also shared a mutual attraction and began to date once a week on a regular basis. There were no demands placed on each other, and in a short period of time began seeing each other several times a week. They discussed in-depth what they wanted out of the relationship. Charles did not feel threatened by Karen, and he did not have the need to push her away.

They had talked about their parents' divorce and their own divorces. They understood each other and both felt that marriage was not the "end-all." Both expressed their need not to marry again and not have more children.

After about a year, Charles and Karen decided to live together. They thought it would be best not to live in either of their apartments. They decided to rent a new apartment that would feel neutral. At this time, they agreed that they only wanted to live together; they would not marry.

This living arrangement worked for both of them. Neither wanted to think of marriage or divorce. They both were open with each other about their issues of trust, loss, and abandonment. They also agreed that neither one of them had totally resolved these issues. As a result, it took some time for them to become comfortable with each other in the same space on a daily basis.

However, with time, both had accepted they made a good decision. Karen and Charles felt they could trust each other. They did go to couple's therapy for a while to help overcome the fears they had. They were able to work through their issues and have become very content with each other. Time has not changed their feelings about each other, and they get along very well. Both Karen and Charles are happy with their decision to live together and marriage is not an issue. They know that this will be their living arrangement for a very long time.

THE OPEN RELATIONSHIP

Norman and Paula have been married for 10 years. They live together on a full-time basis, but they have an open marriage in which periodically they are with other people for quick sexual liaisons and they're both okay with it. When they married, they made an agreement to live this way.

Norman, age 47, is divorced from his first wife of 10 years. He has one child who is grown and living on his own in another state. Norman keeps in contact with his son primarily by phone, but sees him a few times a year.

Norman is an architect, has his own small firm and does well, but he works long hours. He is close with his assistant, Sandy, and spends many hours with her. Occasionally, they will have a drink or dinner together as friends. Their relationship has always been platonic.

Norman began dating in high school and dated a lot of girls during his college years. He did not get into a serious relationship until he met his first wife, Anna. They dated for a short time and then married. Norman felt his marriage was boring, as if he had married his sister. He was not happy so he threw himself into his work and was hardly at home. The marriage lasted 10 years for the sake of their son. However, Norman felt he needed to get divorced even though his son was not grown-up. Anna was not happy, as she still wanted to wait until their son was more mature.

Norman and Anna got along well but had lost the passion they had early in their marriage. Norman wanted to be free again to come and go as he pleased. He also wanted to be with a lot of different women. He had no plans to marry again.

Paula, age 43, had never been married. She dated a lot since college and had several long-term relationships, but none of them lasted over two years. Paula didn't think she wanted to get married, as she feared marriage would ruin a relationship. She had seen too many happy couples become unhappy when they married especially after they had children. Paula wanted continuous excitement in her life and never wanted to fall into a boring routine.

Paula loves her job, which is always exciting, pays well and allows her to be very independent. She works hard and long hours as a designer for women's sportswear. She has been in that business since she was 22 years old and has stayed with the same company. She also had some good friends and didn't mind living alone, but at times, she felt lonely and fantasized about marriage and children. She was very ambivalent, and anyway, there was no one around to marry.

Paula met Norman at a fund-raising party. They both knew a lot of the same people. They had seen each other at several events but the timing always seemed wrong for anything but a nice polite acknowledgement. At this party, they sought each other out to introduce themselves. They talked for several hours—as if they were alone. They were very attracted to each other, and after the party they went out for a drink. Their conversation continued for several more hours. Paula invited Norman back to her house, and they spent the night together. In the morning, Norman asked Paula if she wanted to go to a museum that day. She was excited. They also spent that day together.

Paula and Norman began to see each other almost every night. Norman cut his work hours shorter than usual. They did lots of things together, but the passion they experienced was the best of all. It wasn't much longer, maybe a few months that Norman stayed at Paula's apartment every evening. The relationship was going fast—faster than both had ever imagined. They talked a lot and both knew that they had fallen in love.

As the realization sunk in, Paula began to get a little nervous. She kept thinking about marriage and how marriage had ruined some of her friend's relationships.

She never wanted to lose the passion and intimacy that she had with Norman. She felt the relationship could be headed in that direction and began to feel ambivalent. On the one side, she wanted to marry Norman. On the other side, she felt they needed some distance.

Norman also began to get scared. He hadn't planned on getting this involved and wanted to pull back. They discussed the issue and both agreed not to see each other as often. Paula wanted to go back to three times a week, but Norman didn't want to set a rigid schedule. He just knew that they had gone too far too fast. Norman and Paula tried cutting back the amount of time they saw each other. However, that wasn't working, as they wanted more time together.

The relationship for both of them was too good to be true, and that scared them both. Despite the fear they both had, Norman asked Paula to marry him and she said she would, but Paula again started feeling ambivalent. She needed excitement and wanted to be reassured that their love would always be that way.

She shared her ambivalence with Norman. She also shared with him that the only way she would get married was if they had an "open" relationship. Paula felt if she saw other men, casually not seriously, her relationship with Norman would never get boring. She told him that these relationships might be sexual but would not interfere with their marriage. Norman was somewhat taken back. However, he thought about it and decided that maybe Paula was right. He left his first marriage out of boredom and lack of passion, so he decided he would marry Paula with the agreement of an "open" marriage.

Their marriage has lasted for 10 years. They both feel happy and have accepted their way of life. Paula has gone out and been with other men considerably more than Norman has been seeing other women. He is still comfortable having dinner with his assistant, Sandy, and their relationship still remains platonic. Norman is not upset that Paula goes out more than he does. He is not jealous. Most of the time, they are together and happy. This living arrangement is working well for both of them.

LESS SEPARATE, MORE TOGETHER

Jackie and Robert have been together 13 years, and are not married. They live in separate apartments two days a week and spend five days living together. Wednesday evening Robert goes to Jackie's apartment and stays until Monday morning when he leaves for work. They decided this was the best living arrangement, as Jackie lives in the city and Robert lives about 20 miles out of the city. They follow this arrangement on a regular basis.

Robert, age 48, has never been married. He is a banker at an international bank, with 20 years experience. He enjoys his work and has created extensive personal financial stability.

Robert has three older siblings. His parents have been married for more than half a century and presently reside in a retirement home. Robert is close with his brother and two sisters and sees them fairly frequently.

When Robert is not with Jackie, he usually spends his time alone catching up on his work. Some days he works at the bank into the evening. Robert and Jackie phone each other during the two days they are not together.

Robert began dating during college. He didn't date a lot, as he took college very seriously and studied during the week, dated on weekends.

Until he met Jackie, he had dated a lot of women but only had two other serious relationships. Both lasted about one year. Robert did not want to get married; he didn't want children and decided it would be better to live with someone. He felt marriage was too confining. In fact, both of the women he dated more seriously wanted to get married which doomed both relationships. Robert always felt he needed some time alone during the week. He didn't want any commitments during that time, unless it was his decision.

Jackie is a 46-year-old divorced woman. She was married to Steven for five years. They had no children. Jackie had mixed feelings about getting married. She felt marriage was too confining and she also needed time alone. However, she ignored her needs until she realized that Steven was very demanding of her free time. He was always making plans and on the go. Jackie began to get angry which brought on conflict in the marriage. She began to resent Steven and wanted a divorce.

Jackie is an attorney at a large law firm. She has one younger brother. Her parents had been married for many years until about 10 years ago when her father died. Her mother never remarried and died about a year ago. Jackie had a very difficult time when her mother died. Robert was very supportive, however, she felt the need to join a grief support group.

Jackie and Robert met at the bank used by her law firm. They saw each other several times at the bank when there was a transaction that needed to be completed. It was awkward for Robert but the last time he saw her, he invited Jackie to have a drink with him after work. They enjoyed each other's company saying they would get together again and they began dating. Jackie was comfortable with Robert and found him to be a lot of fun. They dated for several months and the relationship became more serious. The relationship grew stronger and after about a year, Robert wanted to live together. Jackie thought it was a good idea. She suggested they live together five days a week and remain separate in their own apartments the other two days. She also suggested that Robert stay with her, as she lived in the city and it was close to work for both of them. Robert agreed to this arrangement. They both apparently wanted the same living arrangement and both were okay knowing they would probably never marry. It is now 13 years later. Their living arrangement is still the same. Robert looks forward to seeing Jackie on Wednesday, but still needs his two days apart. Jackie feels the same way. Their relationship is a good one—they are both very happy.

"I CAN'T LEAVE HOME"

Angie and Tony have been seeing each other for six years. They get together several times a week. Tony wants Angie to move in with him. He feels that they have known each other long and well enough to take that step. Angie does not want to live with Tony. She lives with her family and can't seem to separate.

Angie, age 35, has never been married. She lives with her parents and her brother Alan who is 37. Neither Angie nor Alan has ever moved away from their parents. They are a very close family. Angie's father has a construction business, is getting older and allows both children to run the business with little involvement on his part. Angie's mother is not physically well. She has numerous medical problems, which often sends her to the hospital. Angie is very involved in the family business. At times, she works late and is unable to see Tony. Eventually, she and her brother will take over the business, which makes her very happy.

Angie's mother is a very controlling woman. She made both children very dependent on her since they were little. Now that she is not well, she is also manipulating Angie and Alan to stay close to her. Both Angie and her brother have been very dependent on their mother. There was a time when Angie couldn't go far from home unless her mother was with her. Angie doesn't question her inability to separate from home and her mother. She does not have a lot of insight and feels it's okay not to want to leave her family. Now that her parents are getting older, it's even more difficult for Angie to separate. She feels they need her to be there for them. Angie does not see moving away from home for a long time.

Tony, age 37, is divorced and has no children. He is a painter and owns the painting company with four employees. He was married for five years to Rosemary. Rosemary was an elementary school teacher. She was dependent on Tony and demanded much of his free time. After a while, Tony began to feel like he was suffocating in his marriage. He tried to get Rosemary interested in other things, but she refused. Tony was very angry, resented her and asked for a divorce. The divorce was not smooth. Rosemary wanted to hang on to the marriage and would not let go. Her dependency needs were too great.

At this time, Tony would like to remarry. His fantasy is that one day Angie will wake up and realize what she's doing is unhealthy—that she needs to separate from her family. He loves her very much and wants to be with her. He is frustrated with their living arrangement, as he feels it is one-sided. However, he has accepted it and will not leave her.

MARRIED AND LIVING TOGETHER

Marcia and Paul are married and live together. They began dating eight years ago and are presently married for five years. They have one child, Sarah, who is two years old.

Marcia is 32 years old and this is her first marriage. Marcia presently works in her own retail store in which she sells baby clothes. She has been working at her store for about four years. She puts in long hours and has a nanny to take care of Sarah. She loves her work, except that she would like to spend more time with Sarah.

Marcia is the youngest of three siblings. She gets along well with her three sisters. They are close and see each other frequently. Marcia's parents live close by and spend as much time as possible with Marcia and her family.

Marcia began dating in high school and continued through college. She had one serious relationship with Adam, which lasted for two years. After college, Adam moved out of state for work. He wanted to marry Marcia, but she didn't feel the same way. She then met Paul and they dated for three years, when they decided to get married. Marcia feels she made the right choice. She is very happy with Paul and they have a good marriage.

Paul is also 32 years old and married for the first time. He is a physician specializing in Pediatric medicine. Paul works long hours, so family time is limited. However, he feels that the time they spend together is quality time. When Sarah was born, he and Marcia had to make some adjustments not only to a new baby but also in their ability to manage their time well. Paul also feels he is in a very good marriage.

Marcia began dating Paul after she finished college. At that time, Paul was still in medical school. Paul spent many hours studying and at the hospital, which made it more difficult to see Marcia. However, when they were together they were happy. They both enjoyed the outdoors, good meals, and quiet romantic times. Marcia was not a demanding person and could easily adjust to Paul's busy schedule. Paul and Marcia dated for several years until they married.

Marcia grew up in a family that seemed quite healthy. Both of her parents were loving and nurturing. She grew up having direction and guidance. She was a happy child.

Paul also grew up in a family that was very supportive and loving. His parents encouraged his desire to become a doctor since the time he was a little boy. He continued to have this wish and they continued to support him.

Marcia and Paul feel very lucky to have met each other. They are compatible on many levels. They get along well and any conflicts that arise are quickly resolved. They communicate well and both are getting their needs met. They both acknowledge that being married and living together is the best arrangement they could possibly have.

Where do you see yourself in the above vignettes? Do you presently have a similar living situation, or are you not at the phase in a relationship? You can recognize that Paul and Marcia really do have a healthy relationship. Angie and Tony appear to be in a no-win situation. The rest of the couples indicate that they are content with their living arrangement. However, it is important to take a look at what might happen if those couples chose to marry and live together. Would they be as happy? The arrangements they have work for them, and there is no need for them to renegotiate—"If it's not broken, don't try and fix it." However, if you were to take a deeper look into those relationships, you might find those involved may have difficulty living any other way. In other words, they may have issues with intimacy and commitment. They may live separately, at least part time, so they don't lose themselves in the relationship due to fears of abandonment. Of course, if these fears exist, they are probably unconscious fears. Thus, you could say these couples found the right place not to experience any unhealthy behavior that could ruin the relationship.

On the other hand, Paul and Marcia are emotionally healthy. No matter what living situation they were in, they would be fine. Neither of them experienced any neglect or trauma as a child and their parents were emotionally available.

CHAPTER 8

Why Is the Honeymoon Over?

People date and sometimes marry. Why is dating so different than being married, or is it? For some people like Marcia and Paul (from the previous chapter) it isn't. For others described throughout the book, being married can bring on a new set of problems.

Reading this book in its entirety will show you how to be in a healthy relationship. Through the knowledge and insight you gain, you will have what you need to succeed in a relationship.

However, it is important to recognize that people who have difficulty with relationships may have difficulty in a marriage. You succeed in attaining your goal, which is to be in a loving relationship. Then you may decide to marry. Marriage is an "official" totally committed relationship. What if you develop anxiety about becoming too attached? Those feelings may emerge just as they did when you began your relationship.

Issues not totally resolved can rear their ugly head when married. Fears can come back. Anxiety and depression may return. Old behaviors begin to take over. You wonder how you reverted back when you were doing so well.

It is common for people with long-term issues regarding relationships to see these issues reemerge once they get married. Being married is like "going home again," as you have now become a family. Unconsciously, you may begin to revert back to old behaviors, which were very uncomfortable and painful when you were a child living at home. But remember! If you overcame these issues before, you can overcome them again. You've already read the book, are able to be in a healthy relationship and most likely will be able to sustain a healthy marriage. Now you may have to reread this book to polish up on your skills.

The following cases illustrate the emotional and behavioral changes that can occur when a relationship goes from dating to marriage.

BARBARA AND PHILIP

Barbara is a 40-year-old woman who married Philip six months ago. This is her first marriage. Barbara began dating in college; however, her relationships never lasted longer than six months. When people would ask her why she never married, she would say it was because she "never met the right man." Barbara was getting tired of being asked about marriage. Her family and relatives wondered why "such a pretty girl could never find the right man." Her friends, by this time, knew that any relationship Barbara was in would probably not last.

Barbara had been in a lot of relationships thinking each one would end up in marriage—each one did end, but not in marriage. She found herself in love but her boyfriends, for the most part, broke up with her. She was usually surprised, as her relationships seemed to be going well. And, after each breakup, Barbara was devastated. Barbara needed to be in a relationship or she wasn't happy. She always felt a big void unless there was someone in her life.

Barbara was in her thirties when she realized something was going wrong with all her relationships. She eventually understood that each of the men she chose was not able to commit. Her friends told her over the years that she was choosing the wrong men, but Barbara didn't listen. When she did choose someone who was emotionally distant, she felt that she had the power to change him, so he would be able to be close and commit. Barbara knew she was attractive and smart and believed in each relationship that the man she was with would never leave her or want to be with anyone else. She learned later rather than sooner that she was again "driving down the wrong road."

It wasn't until she met Philip that she thought her dream might finally come true. Barbara met Philip through a dating service. Phillip was a really nice guy who treated her very well. He was attentive, called when he said he would and seemed able to make a commitment. After several months of dating, Barbara was concerned about Phillip's moods. Philip was moody and, at times, there was no getting through to him. He went into his own little world and came out when he was ready. Barbara didn't worry about it, as he always came around. She felt she could handle his distancing behavior.

Barbara and Philip dated for about six months, and then Barbara told Philip she wanted to get married. She told him if she was going to have any children, now was the time to do it. It was already getting late and she didn't want to have to adopt. Philip was very hesitant; he loved Barbara, and although he didn't feel ready to get married, he too thought it was a good time in his life to take that step. Philip went back and forth for a while changing his mind about marriage; he was ambivalent and it took about a month before he could make a commitment. He finally told Barbara that he would marry her, and both of them seemed very happy.

Barbara has been a registered nurse for 15 years. She presently works in the intensive care unit at a large city hospital. She was up for promotions several times, but due to her emotional instability around her relationships, she never received a promotion.

Barbara has one older sister who apparently has also had problems with relationships. Her sister is still single. Both Barbara and her sister were not very happy as children. They felt unloved and as if they were growing up by themselves. Their mother was physically present but not emotionally demonstrative. Their father, who was cold and distant, worked long hours and was not home much of the time. The relationship between their parents was not close. Barbara and her sister didn't see much affection between them, although they were nice and polite to each other. If there were problems between them, they tried to hide them from their children.

Philip is also 40 years old and this is his first marriage. Philip is an accountant with his own firm. He is financially secure, as his business has done well. He has had his own firm for the last five years. Prior to having his own company, he worked for two other accounting firms where he did quite well.

Philip began dating in college. He felt he couldn't get serious with anyone until he finished college and earned his CPA. Philip had several long-term relationships, which he would end when he felt the woman wanted to marry him. He also felt he hadn't met the right person. He was not aware that he had problems with intimacy and commitment until he went for therapy. He was then able to recognize his difficulties in his relationships. When he met Barbara, he felt very comfortable, however, he still had some need to distance. He knew Barbara was very special and didn't want to lose her because of his issues, so he worked hard in therapy.

Philip is the middle child with an older brother and younger sister. His parents were good to him and he believed he was getting the love he needed. However, it wasn't until he was in therapy years later, when he realized his mother was not as loving as he wanted to believe. She was distant and most of her attention went to his father. Philip's father was somewhat passive and went along with everything his wife wanted. He did not have the ability to be close with his children even though he spent time with them.

After their wedding, Barbara and Philip headed for the Caribbean for their honeymoon. It wasn't long after their honeymoon that Barbara's behavior began to change. She became moody, distant and did not want to be as close to Philip as she was prior to their marriage. She didn't understand her behavior, as she knew she loved Philip. She just felt this need to be away from him. She began making more plans with her friends. Philip wasn't upset about her seeing her friends, however, he was concerned about Barbara's behavior. He wondered if she was going to stay distant or if she would move closer to him. Barbara became defensive when Philip asked what was going on. Since she didn't understand her own behavior, how could she discuss it with Philip? It was as if their roles changed once they married. Barbara had become emotionally unavailable.

If you take a look at Barbara's family, you will see that no one was close. Barbara chose unavailable men to try to change them into loving men who could commit. Her unconscious need was to reenact the relationships she had with her father and mother, and what she was doing was trying to make them more loving and available. She was acting out old familiar problems thinking she had the power to change things. However, she couldn't change them as a child and was not going to change them as an adult.

Barbara was not aware that she feared intimacy, as she never had it. However, when Philip became emotionally available, Barbara got scared and had to back off. She did not know what it was like to be intimate and committed, and if she got what she thought she wanted, she feared losing it. Thus, in looking at the above dynamics, you could say that someone who is emotionally unavailable to his or her partner who is available may be emotionally available to another partner who is unavailable.

AMANDA AND LAWRENCE

Amanda, 26 years old, has been married to Lawrence for two years. This is Amanda's first marriage. Amanda began dating in high school.

She was very popular and many of the boys wanted to date her. She dated a lot but didn't take anyone seriously. She was consumed in her studies, as she wanted to go to law school and become an attorney.

Amanda met Lawrence through her parents. Her mother knew Lawrence's mother through her bridge club. Amanda and Lawrence felt awkward, as they would have rather met on their own. When they got to know each other, they weren't sorry about their parents' intervention. They really liked each other a lot and began dating on a frequent basis. At the time they began to date, Amanda was finishing law school. She felt comfortable about where she was in her studies, and felt it was the right time to date seriously. Amanda and Lawrence continued to date and after about a year, they began thinking about getting married. Both of them felt ready to take this big step, however, Amanda still hadn't finished law school, and after graduation she knew she would have to study for the BAR exam. Therefore, she felt she needed to make some decisions with Lawrence about how they would manage their lives. Amanda was someone who needed to have structure with her career goals. She needed to work on a schedule which meant that she and Lawrence would have to discuss the ways in which she could meet his and her own needs. Amanda and Lawrence were able to communicate well. They were good listeners and problem solvers. This took a load off of Amanda who felt the marriage would not infringe on her studies, and she felt comfortable getting married. She was very excited about marrying Lawrence and she was also very excited about becoming an attorney. At that time, she didn't want to think about having children—that would come later.

Lawrence, age 27, is an attorney. He recently joined a corporate law firm. He loves his work and is working long hours. He wants to get ahead with the hope that one day he would become a partner in the firm.

Lawrence didn't begin to date until college. He was not very serious about dating. It was just something fun to do when he wasn't involved in his studies.

Lawrence has one older brother who is also an attorney. His father is also an attorney. As a child, Lawrence would become upset, as his father worked long hours and sometimes on the weekend. Lawrence played baseball and felt like he didn't even have a father, because his father never had time to go to any of his games. Lawrence was not very close to his mother. They argued a lot, which made it difficult for him to feel close to her.

It was several months into the marriage when Lawrence found himself feeling angry with Amanda. He was feeling like he didn't have a wife, as she seemed more involved with her studies than with him. Even though they discussed her studying prior to getting married, he didn't seem to care, as he wanted her attention. Amanda would get mad at Lawrence when he expressed his anger. She felt like he was attacking her. She tried to talk to him but he wasn't listening. He couldn't even repeat what she said, which meant she couldn't talk to him. Lawrence became even more angry accusing Amanda of not being available to take care of the household chores. This was also discussed prior to the marriage and Amanda felt she was doing her share. They found each other attacking. Their communication was becoming destructive to the marriage. Amanda found she couldn't concentrate and Lawrence was not functioning at the same level at his job. Both began to feel depressed—the marriage was beginning to feel hopeless.

It appears that Lawrence had a great deal of repressed anger toward both of his parents. Since he couldn't express that anger to his parents, he held it in for many years.

As the marriage progressed, the anger began to emerge and Lawrence began to transfer that anger to Amanda. Amanda became the target for his anger, which was really toward his parents.

NANCY AND CARL

Nancy, age 34 and Carl, age 37 dated for two years prior to getting married. They were both in love and their relationship was satisfying. Prior to this relationship, both had problems with intimacy. Nancy felt that Carl was emotionally distant. However, Carl became less distant once he recognized this and worked hard to overcome this problem. Carl thought, at times Nancy would hold back sexually. However, when Nancy felt more trusting of Carl, she didn't have a problem. The relationship went well until they got married.

Nancy and Carl are presently married for two years. The relationship was going well until about six months into the marriage, when Nancy began to argue with Carl on a regular basis. At times, Carl felt Nancy was being irrational and there was no way to talk to her when she would pick these arguments. Nancy would argue about small things that had no major relevance. This left both of them at a distance from each other and they didn't speak to each other for hours or even a day.

Nancy, not consciously, needed to distance from Carl, so she created these arguments. What she was trying to do was to sabotage the marriage by pushing Carl away—and it worked! However, once she successfully pushed him away, she was able to be close to him again. Carl started to feel like he was in a "push-pull" or "come here–go away" relationship. Nancy's behavior continued for about another six months, until Carl began to feel angry.

Nancy did not resort to this behavior while they were dating, only because Carl was emotionally distant. His distancing did not bring up her issues with closeness. However, now that he is able to be closer, Nancy gets scared and feels trapped.

Nancy and Carl both worked on helping Nancy to express her fear and need to sabotage. By expressing her fears, they were brought to her consciousness and she became aware of her need to work on this problem. Nancy was able to make some connection to this problem by looking at her family dynamics when she was young. She realized she distanced to protect herself from her parents who couldn't be close. She knew her parents could not meet her emotional needs. With some insight and behavioral work, Nancy was able to stop this behavior within a few months.

CELESTE AND PETER

Celeste, age 33 and Peter, age 31 have been married for one year. They dated for a year before they got married. This is a second marriage for both of them with neither of them having any children from their first marriages. Celeste was married for two years and the relationship ended in a divorce. Peter got divorced after three years of marriage.

Celeste works as a producer for a small film company. She has worked at this job for eight years. Celeste worked hard and had little time for social events. In fact, she felt so independent that she was not interested in meeting someone or getting married again. She had a few close friends who she saw on occasion.

Celeste was very independent and comfortable with being alone. In her "down time," she would read mystery books and actually enjoyed getting away from the reality of a hard day's work. Celeste gets along well with her one sister who is four years older and they try to see each other fairly often. Celeste's parents were loving and caring, however, they both passed away from cancer when Celeste was in her late teens. Celeste and her sister had a very difficult time with the loss of their parents. Her father died when she was seventeen and her mother died when she was nineteen. Celeste was particularly close to her father spending a lot of time with him going to various events. She was also close to her mother and they spent their time together having lunch and shopping for clothes.

Peter is an engineer and has worked for the same firm for 10 years. His job keeps him very busy. Prior to dating Celeste, he dated several different women. He wanted to marry again but couldn't find the right person until he met Celeste.

Peter comes from a large, close family. He has two younger brothers and two younger sisters, all geographically close, and they see each other fairly often. His parents are close to the children. Peter feels that as a child, his parents were kind and loving. Everyone seemed to get along well most of the time.

Celeste met Peter at a restaurant. Celeste was having dinner with two of her friends when Peter approached her. At first, she was not interested in talking to him, however she found him to be nice and polite. He invited her for a drink after she finished dinner with her friends and she accepted. They began dating regularly. Celeste was uncomfortable with seeing Peter so often. She felt she didn't have the time, however she enjoyed his company, eventually fell in love with him, and they dated until they married.

Celeste and Peter felt they were happily married and even pondered over the thought of having children. It was about three months into the marriage when Celeste's behavior began to change. She started calling Peter at work several times a day. If he had to leave town, she would have severe anxiety. She felt that if he left, he wouldn't come back. Celeste began to act like a dependent child. She didn't understand her need to be so dependent but felt like she had changed and couldn't help herself. She was so independent—what was happening to her now?

Peter was puzzled by her behavior and started to feel suffocated. He felt he couldn't do anything without Celeste being by his side—like a little girl being with her father. Celeste actually regressed to being a little girl with her father. Peter was her husband but did not care for his new role.

It appears that Celeste was traumatized by the death of both of her parents. She remembers she was very upset at the time and felt she appropriately grieved. However, at this time, there appeared to be some unresolved issues. Celeste's need to be so independent was, in fact, a way for her not to have to deal with her strong dependency needs. She was not consciously aware of her need to be so independent, but instead, her behavior was clearly independent.

Peter initially resented Celeste being so dependent. He began to accept it but was not happy. Celeste was not happy with her behavior and decided to seek treatment to help her with her unresolved grief. She saw a therapist for about two months and felt that she was again living in the present. She became more independent and their life returned to a healthy adult love.

RICHARD AND COURTNEY

Richard, age 42 and Courtney, age 38 began dating five years ago. They are presently married for two years. Both Richard and Courtney have been married once before and are both divorced. Richard has one child and Courtney has two children from their previous marriages.

Richard works for himself. He owns a gourmet wine and grocery shop. He has owned the store for 10 years and is doing very well. He is very good with his customers giving them excellent service. He is also well known in the community and appears to be well liked.

Richard is an only child. He grew up in the same neighborhood where his store is located. He was married when he was much younger, had one child and he divorced after five years. His son lived with his mother, which worked out well. Richard saw his son one day a week and every other weekend. They got along fairly well except Richard was hard on his son concerning his studies. His son had not been doing well in school.

Richard's mother is close to him and Courtney. She visits a great deal. It seems like she likes to be away from home as much as she can. When Richard was a child, she was physically present but was not emotionally demonstrative. His father always worked hard and was away from home most of the day. As a child, Richard remembers that his father was very bossy. He was always telling the family what to do and how to do it. He was very controlling. As a result, Richard's mother became submissive and let her husband run the home and her life.

Courtney is a college professor. She teaches history at a nearby college. She has been teaching for 11 years. Courtney has one older brother. They do not see each other except for a few times a year, mostly on holidays. Courtney has joint custody of her two children. They live with her most of the time. Her children like Richard, but they don't feel like he is their dad. He does not seem to make quality time to be with both of them. This bothers Courtney, but she defends Richard because of his long work hours.

Courtney describes her childhood as fairly happy. She was closer to her father than her mother. Courtney spent a lot of time with her father. He is a very kind, loving, and considerate man. She describes her mother as a warm person, but was upset with her mother a great deal of the time. It seems that Courtney's mother was always telling Courtney and her brother what to do. She was not a good listener and wanted everything done her way. If you didn't listen to her, she could be punitive, which was hurtful to Courtney and her brother.

Courtney began dating in high school. She was not serious with anyone until she met her ex-husband. They married young and had two children early in their marriage. It seems like they didn't have enough time to really attach in the marriage because of the children, which left them both with an empty feeling. It was difficult for them to get close and they ultimately divorced.

Richard and Courtney met through a mutual friend. They liked each other immediately and began dating. Richard was good to Courtney. He was kind, sincere, and gentle. Courtney felt good about herself when with Richard. She felt very lucky to have met him. He too, felt like he was very lucky to have Courtney in his life. Richard liked Courtney's children and treated them well. Courtney, in turn, had positive feelings about Richard's son. Richard and Courtney dated for several years and then married.

It wasn't long after they married that Richard began to want things his way. He did not really listen to what Courtney wanted. He became very controlling and Courtney began to feel like she didn't have a say in the marriage. Prior to their marriage, he seemed very different. They always talked about how things should be done. They felt they had to negotiate when it came to the children, and they were always able to compromise. Now, Richard didn't even know the word compromise.

Courtney was not going to become submissive. She realized that she had become her mother and Richard took on his father's role. She was determined not to be like her mother. She was also determined to take back some power giving Richard less power in the relationship. She began to feel stronger and became more independent of

Richard, and as a result, Richard began to calm down and become less controlling. He realized that he no longer could control Courtney and reverted back to himself as he was around the time they were dating. Courtney continued to empower herself and the relationship between Courtney and Richard became more equal.

CHAPTER 9
Men and Women

Finding the right partner is obviously intrinsic to the building of a healthy relationship. It is possible, however, to find the communication between you and that "right" partner is less than satisfying. You ponder whether your partner is the "right" person for you. You care for your partner, however, you are not aware of precisely what to do to change your patterns of communication. Situations vary. You can begin to communicate more constructively. For some couples, regardless of what they are taught, they remain in old unhealthy patterns, which can cause communication to be impossible. Remaining in old unhealthy patterns is a common problem. Frequently, one of you feels you are perfectly fine in the way you communicate, and do not need to learn new communication tools. Often, one of you will not acknowledge or be accountable for any problem. Instead, you will blame it on your partner.

JACK AND MARCIA

Jack, age 55, and Marcia, age 49 have been married for three years. Both of them were divorced and have grown children. Jack and Marcia met through a long distance matchmaking service and dated for two years prior to marrying. The courting part of their relationship was wonderful. Most of the time Marcia would travel to see Jack because business necessitated his being out of town for most of the week. During those two years, there was no perceived problem with communication. They decided to marry and Marcia moved in with Jack. They began working on their house through construction of new additions and updating of old features. Jack had one child who spent several days a week with him. Marcia had four children living out of state. They were welcome to visit often. In fact, they were invited to live with her and Jack. Eventually two of her children accepted and moved in with them.

Jack and Marcia began having problems as soon as they got married. Most of the problems were related to communication. In fact, Jack and Marcia really did not communicate. Jack was someone who thought he was right about everything and everyone. If he were challenged, he could rationalize everything he said to the point that Marcia just gave up. However, she did not give up without trying to get him to understand what she was saying. It was almost as if he didn't get it or he couldn't understand what Marcia was saying. Jack was so insecure and so well defended that no one could get through to him unless it was through agreement with him. Apparently, he had never developed relating skills even though he owned an antique store and had to relate to people all-day and everyday. Yet, conversations with his customers were short and sweet. He would be charming when it came to selling something. His focus was more on business than it was on his relationship with Marcia. Prior to their marriage, Jack set up a prenuptial agreement, so in the event of a divorce, Marcia would get nothing. Ostensibly, he did this to be sure Marcia was not marrying him for his money. He also felt that if Marcia wanted anything, she would have to pay for it herself. Marcia only had a part-time job that gave her a small salary.

Marcia became frustrated soon after they were married. She uprooted for this marriage and was determined to make it work. She loved Jack, and good times were abundant. In fact, Jack could be very sweet, but in a childlike way. At times, Marcia felt like she was living with two different people. This only made things more difficult for her, as she didn't know who he really was. Overall, Marcia felt that the bad times outweighed the good. This was a sign that this was not a good relationship. Conversations between them usually escalated into sparring matches. It was as if they were each alone in their communication and neither of them heard the other. If Jack were angry about something Marcia did, he would attack her. She would try to explain. However, it didn't matter. He thought what he thought and nothing she could say would make him less angry. Many times their arguments escalated and became volatile. They would be mean to each other with continual attacks made toward the other. They would react not respond. These arguments would end with both of them still being angry and not talking to each other. The only time Jack would apologize would be when he wanted to have sex.

Jack wanted to have sex to please himself. He had no real interest in pleasing Marcia. He also wanted sex when he wanted it. He would be furious if she refused him. Marcia tried to explain the importance of affection as well as the importance of her own pleasure while having sex. In response, Jack would please her, but he always retreated to his previous patterns. Marcia also wanted Jack to be more affectionate outside the bedroom. Jack did not feel the need to be emotionally demonstrative.

In looking at this marriage, it appears that nothing is working. There are many reasons for both of their behaviors. Jack has never left his past emotionally. As a result of childhood issues, Jack is narcissistic, insecure, and guarded. He never learned how to love in an honest and direct way. And his biggest issue is trust. From his present behavior, it appears that as a child, Jack was deprived of the necessary skills to learn to attach to someone when he became an adult. Jack's inability to meet Marcia's needs on just about every level has left Marcia thinking about divorce on a regular basis. However, Marcia is still in denial. She will think about divorce and then she will rationalize Jack's behavior. In her denial, she really believes that Jack will change. At times, she believes when things are bad that it is her fault. This only adds to her denial. Marcia is by no means perfect. There are times when she refuses to recognize her part in the relationship. She also has difficulty relating and communicating in an honest direct manner. Marcia also has a pronounced lack of trust resulting from conflicts within her family of origin.

Marcia and Jack say they care for each other. However, their behavior says the opposite. There is little chance for either of them to experience a healthy satisfying relationship. However, this does not mean they will get a divorce. If they are stuck in their childhood, they will continue patterns that are familiar even if they are destructive and painful. They will continue in those patterns and not make any changes in their marriage.

This example is to show you that not every relationship will benefit from understanding and learning new ways to relate. If one person is not willing to change their patterns and take any risks, there is nothing that can be done to help the relationship. Jack would have to be in a great deal of emotional distress before he might even take a look at his behavior. Even so, he would be more likely to blame his emotional state on external factors. What makes it worse, is the fact that Jack is aware of Marcia's difficulty communicating. It then becomes easier for him to blame their lack of communication on her.

GENDER DIFFERENCES

There are defined biological and environmental differences between men and women. The socialization process is also different. Think about the way boys and girls are taught to behave as children. Boys are taught not to express emotions. This is not true of all boys, but at some point during childhood, they will learn through their peers that being emotional is unacceptable. On the other hand, it is expected that girls will be emotional. The differences in boys and girls will grow into differences between men and women. Again these differences vary. Some men and women are emotionally similar in that both can express feelings. But for the most part, we cannot ignore the differences, which can be emotional, physical, and sexual.

Men, who have difficulty expressing emotion, may use sex as an emotional outlet and desire more frequently then some women. A desire to have sex does not necessarily translate to being emotional with their partner. Women usually welcome affection outside the bedroom as well as during sex; many men do not seek that kind of affection and are content with just the sexual act.

An area, in which you can see a big difference between the sexes, is in the way men and woman deal with being emotionally upset. Men tend to keep their feelings to themselves. They may create other outlets such as playing sports or working on projects as a way to cope with their emotions. Many men work a great deal of the time in order not to feel or to get away from what they are feeling. Women need to express their feelings and they want their partner to respond. The following are typical examples of confronting what may appear as a common, simple situation.

Heidi: "I feel very sad today."

Daniel: "Don't feel sad."

Heidi: "I can't help it."

Daniel: "Why don't you go out for a drink with your friends? You'll feel better."

In the above example, Daniel is doing what men typically do. He doesn't want to deal with Heidi's emotions. He thinks to help her is to tell her what to feel and to tell her how to fix it. Men like to solve the problem. It is inherent in their nature to be concrete about things even as it extends to being concrete in an abstract situation.

Heidi would have liked for Daniel to respond different. Here is an example:

Heidi: "I feel very sad today."
Daniel: "I'm sorry. What's bothering you?"
Heidi: "I don't know."
Daniel: "Well, lets talk about it. Maybe we can find out what's going on."

As mentioned earlier, couples have different personalities, which will have an affect on how they communicate. It will also affect how they deal with conflict. The following is one example.

Eric: "Nancy, I don't have a clean shirt to wear tomorrow!"
Nancy: "I'm sorry. I'll wash one."
Eric: "What is the matter with you?"
Nancy: "I will wash it right now."

Eric is angry that he doesn't have a shirt to wear. His anger may be legitimate. However, he presents it to Nancy in a hostile way, which puts Nancy on the defensive. Nancy is generally passive and defensive in her communication. Eric takes advantage of Nancy's passivity by speaking to her in a way that conveys disrespect. If Nancy learned to be less defensive and less passive, the conversation might look like this.

Eric: "Nancy, I don't have a clean shirt to wear tomorrow!"
Nancy: " I was so busy, I didn't get to do the laundry. Why don't I wash one for you now?"
Eric: "Okay."
Nancy: "Working part-time and taking care of the chores can be overwhelming at times."
Eric: "I know."

In this example, Nancy states why she didn't get to do the laundry. Eric may still be annoyed, however, he is more responsive than reactive in his communication. Nancy is less passive and more direct.

If both partners are passive or indirect, neither one wants to upset the other. They are both holding on to their feelings. The conflicts are still alive but there are no resolutions. These situations may lead to resentment, building up unresolved conflicts, which will eventually manifest in behaviors that could hurt the relationship. An example of this type of interaction might be:

Ed: "I don't have a shirt to wear today."
Sherry: "Oh."
Ed: "Well that's okay, I will wear the same shirt I wore yesterday."
Sherry: "Okay."

The following is an example in which there is all reaction and no responsiveness. Both of them find it easier to hold on to their anger. They are aggressive in their interactions. The following example may show a couple with each being more comfortable with distancing behaviors.

Paul: "I don't have a clean shirt to wear today! You are getting lazier all the time!"
Terry: "Me Lazy! You're the lazy one. You never do anything around the house."
Paul: "You don't know what you're talking about, and I need a shirt to wear."
Terry: " Well, wash it yourself. Maybe it will teach you a lesson."

Reacting and responding are words, which clearly reveal how people communicate. Reacting takes no thought. Reacting is impulsive in which you do not think about what or how you are expressing yourself. In reacting, you express no consideration for your partner. It does not matter to you what effect it has on your partner. During those times, you can't get past your own needs. Continually reacting will lead to further conflicts and an unsatisfactory relationship.

Responding, on the other hand, takes thought. Responding considers the other person and their needs. Responding allows your needs to be heard and be met. The next chapter "Practice Makes Perfect" provides further information on the concepts of reacting and responding.

The following may help clarify the difference between reacting and responding:

Answer Yes or No to the following statements:

My family was not interactive.
   Yes   No

My family argued a lot.
   Yes   No

When angry, a member of my family would verbally attack another member.
Yes   No

Arguments were never handled quietly in my family.
Yes   No

I come from a chaotic family where members would yell and scream to be heard.
Yes   No

Reacting is a healthy response to anger.
Yes   No

I find it difficult to express my feelings without reacting.
Yes   No

I do not understand the difference between reacting and responding.
Yes   No

I am unclear as to the difference in beginning my statements with "I" or "You."
Yes   No

I think I should just say what I want to without thinking about how my partner will feel.
Yes   No

If you answered "yes" to four or more questions, it indicates that it is important for you to learn and understand the difference between reacting and responding. Depending on whether you are reacting or responding, differing interactions will be generated between you and your partner. The importance here is that being reactive can be very destructive to a relationship while being responsive will only enhance your relationship.

An excellent example of the differences between reacting and responding would be the use "you" or "I" at the beginning of your statements. "You" or "I" will determine the outcome of what you say. If you want a response from your partner, you must present your statement in a way that will not put them on the defensive. If you begin your sentence with "you," you will put the other person on the defensive and create a reactive response. These statements usually begin with "you." If you want a responsive answer to a question or statement, you need to begin your sentences with "I."

The concepts of reacting or responding should not be difficult to understand. Examples in this book will clarify the differences. This concept is a significant part of communication. Your relationship will suffer when you or your partner are being reactive. Changing from being reactive to being responsive takes practice. You may want to ask a friend to practice this with you, and while it may not be comfortable at first, it will become so with practice.

When you respond you are listening to how your partner feels. You take into consideration those feelings and respond to them.

Ann: "I am looking forward to having dinner alone with you tonight."

Stan: "Don't you remember I told you I had a business dinner this evening?"

Ann: "I guess I forgot or maybe you didn't mention it. But I will miss you."

Stan: "It doesn't really matter whose fault it is. But I know you're disappointed. Can we have dinner alone tomorrow night?"

Ann: "Yes, I would like that very much."

Stan: "I'm sorry if there was a miscommunication."

Ann: "So am I."

The above is an example of a couple who can communicate in a very constructive manner. Their use of responding is repeated a number of times in their dialogue and clearly shows a good understanding of this concept.

There are some interactions in which one partner is unable to tolerate conflict. That partner reacts in a manner where they are listening, but won't say anything. This is not responding. This is avoidance—communication that can lead to further avoidant conflicts. This vignette is similar to one given above, however, more extreme.

Diane: "I wasn't happy with the way you treated me last night."

Jim: (acknowledges by moving his head)

Diane: "Please don't do that again."

Jim: (acknowledges again by moving his head)

This type of reaction from Jim would no doubt make Diane more upset. She cannot tell whether he is really listening. And if he is, he is not really responding. Diane wants to discuss what happened. Jim doesn't. She knows if she continues talking about the way she feels, he will only react with the same kind of answers. She doesn't want to get angry with him, as it is likely that he won't respond. This would only create more conflict, so she lets it go. This works for Jim, but not for Diane. This type of relating is unproductive and will not allow the relationship to grow.

There are, of course, healthy interactions in which both partners respond in an assertive manner as indicated in the example of Ann and Stan mentioned earlier. An essential element in achieving constructive and productive interactions is to be able to respond in an assertive way. As you have seen in the former chapter, couples can learn to let go of unproductive ways of relating. Learning and practicing new skills will enable couples to listen to each other and respond in a way in which conflicts will get resolved. The above examples show couples that have learned and have been using the same ways to communicate for many years. Breaking patterns can be difficult, however not impossible. Motivation and practice is the key to successful interaction.

Many of you ask yourself whether or not to choose a relationship in which your partner is like you or the opposite or maybe somewhere in between. The answer is it really doesn't make a difference as long as you are happy in your relationship. You may find that communication would be different depending on your choice. If someone is more like you, it may be easier to talk. Your understanding of what your partner is saying may not involve long explanations. Your partner may understand you immediately. There also may be fewer conflicts to resolve. It is not uncommon for people to feel bored with someone similar to themselves. They like the excitement that can come with someone who is different. However, this varies for most people. Again, there is no right answer. What is important is that you learn and apply productive skills to your ways of relating. No matter how you do it or the time it takes, if it's productive, your relationship will have a much better chance at being successful.

OPPOSITES ATTRACT

We have all heard the phrase "opposites attract." There may be some truth to this phrase, but, again, it does not mean that you cannot be attracted to someone who is more like you. Attractions are all different and based on needs that will vary. However, again, it is important to understand your own dynamics and recognize if your attraction is for healthy reasons. You may keep finding yourself attracted to someone who is different, and those relationships may not have worked for you. It's possible that you may need to find some-one who is a little more like yourself.

NEIL AND LINDA

Neil, age 30, is presently dating Linda, age 28. They have been dat-ing for about two years. Neil's physical appearance is the opposite of Linda's. He is also emotionally very different. Neil with dark hair and dark eyes was very attracted to Linda's blond hair and blue eyes. Neil who was quiet and not emotional was attracted to Linda who was extroverted and emotional. It was easy for Linda to express her feelings. At times, she could be over reactive and become too emo-tional. Yet, Neil was attracted to all of it, because he had difficulty with his emotions. He was not emotional and had difficulty expressing his feelings. Sometimes, when opposites attract, one person feels like they are missing something that their partner has. You could say by being connected to your partner, you can live vicariously through them. Linda represents the person who can feel for Neil. Neil identi-fies with Linda's ability to feel. Opposites take in what the other has to offer and it becomes theirs as well. Neil feels his feelings through Linda, and therefore, doesn't have to feel them himself.

Sometimes what starts off as an attraction to the opposite person, can change to resentment toward that person. Neil is presently begin-ning to resent Linda's continual emotive state. It has become annoy-ing and no longer attractive to him. In essence, in many situations in which opposites attract, the initial attraction, which was positive, has now become negative. Linda, as well, is also beginning to feel different toward Neil.

She saw his being quiet and reserved as being stable and secure. She felt protected from her own emotional states, and felt more stable identifying with Neil. However, now Linda complains that Neil is boring. She feels he is introverted and never wants to do anything.

The above example is not always the case. There are opposites who are attracted for similar reasons. However, the differences may not become a problem. Neil and Linda can learn to work through and resolve their issues by recognizing what the issues are, identifying their goals and learning the skills to meet these goals. For example, Neil and Linda may have a goal that involves him being more social and her being less dramatic. This is definitely a goal that can be achieved.

It may not be as simple as it sounds, yet, motivation and willingness to make changes, can be rewarded with a satisfying long-term relationship.

CHANGING RELATIONSHIPS

The lack of verbal and physical communication can be an issue for couples especially if they have been together over a long period of time. This can gradually occur as time passes; your career changes and your children have grown up. Sometimes, when all your children leave home, you are left with an empty feeling. You probably heard of the phrase the "Empty Nest Syndrome." Some couples realize that most of their relationship was around their work and children. They had mutual goals. However, when only the two of you are left, you may feel the need to begin to take a new road. That road can be taken together or alone.

Some people begin to develop friendships that are separate from the marriage. They may develop separate interests. They begin to live their life as separate people. It may not include a life together even if you choose to stay married. If both partners mutually agree to live their lives separately there may not be a problem. However, if one-person feels the need for a closer relationship, the couple needs to begin discussing what their individual needs are in the marriage. If one person wants to see a change and the other doesn't want to upset the status quo, conflict will emerge. Whatever the issues, the couple needs to redefine their marriage and to discuss their individual needs as well as their needs in the marriage. Together, they need to set goals which include new behaviors that are realistic. Motivation to make the necessary changes to achieve these goals, will result in a more satisfying relationship.

JOE AND SHARON

Joe and Sharon, both are 62, have been married for 30 years. They did not get married young, and both of them were doing well being single. Both had good jobs and were independent financially and socially. When they met, they were both hesitant about making a long-term commitment, as they liked their lives the way they were. Entering a relationship caused each of them to feel they were suffocating and losing their freedom. However, they dated and after two years they decided to marry. At the time they married, they were convinced that it was what they wanted.

After being married for about 20 years, Joe and Sharon began doing things independent of the other. Other than their professional lives, they had developed separate friendships as well as interests.

The time spent together was not quality time. It was more like the time was filling in the spaces on their calendars. They continued in this way for a number of years. Neither of them complained. Both seemed content.

It was not until Joe began to feel dissatisfied that he told Sharon he wanted to discuss their relationship. Joe was beginning to feel the need to be close. He liked his life, but he felt something was missing. He realized he missed his close relationship with Sharon. He was feeling the lack of both verbal and physical communication. Sharon told him he was just having a rough time and things would get better. She acted as if he was having a problem on his own, which really wasn't her responsibility. Joe felt that Sharon was not listening to what he wanted and needed, as she was very comfortable in the life she was leading. Joe was having a difficult time not being heard, so he decided to go into therapy. As a result, it appeared that Joe felt like he lost Sharon. He felt if she wasn't coming back, he needed to leave the marriage. The therapist encouraged that Joe and Sharon enter into conjoint marital sessions. Joe agreed. Sharon was not interested.

Joe decided to ask Sharon for a divorce. She, in turn, thought he was being ridiculous. Sharon was not listening and was not going to be threatened with a divorce. In fact, she didn't believe him and went about her life as usual. Joe began the process of divorce. It was not until then, that Sharon was able to remove herself from her world that didn't include Joe. She was shocked at the idea of divorce. At first, she thought it would be for the best. She later began to feel ambivalent and did not know which route to take. She felt she needed therapy to help her clarify her goals and work through issues that would interfere with meeting those goals. In therapy, Sharon realized that after her children left home, she was lost. By that time, some distance had developed between her and Joe. She was at a loss in trying to bring some closeness to the relationship. It was easier for her to create more distance. Sharon recognized that she did have deep caring feelings for Joe. She began to think about how they initially became more separate, and she began to identify what kept them moving further apart. She realized that they had stopped any real communication at one point and were never motivated to work on their issues. It was not until now that she realized her life was not all she thought it was. She also recognized that they were going to have to start at the beginning in building a new relationship. Previously, they did have good communication and there were not many conflicts that couldn't be resolved fairly easily. Both Sharon and Joe began spending more time together. They sought marital counseling to help them make this transition easier. Before they would feel comfortable together, they needed to recognize and work on resolving the issues that pulled them apart. Their communication was constructive and positive. They knew how to respond to each other and there was little reacting. Although it took some time, Joe and Sharon began to find themselves in a relationship that was mutually satisfying.

After a period of time in the marriage, Joe and Sharon chose not to continue to be intimate. This is quite different from those of you who are not yet at a place where you feel you have a choice. There may be those of you who are unable and have problems with closeness. These problems may involve difficulty expressing thoughts, feelings, and needs. It may also involve difficulty in expressing physical closeness. When couples have these difficulties, it usually indicates the fear of both intimacy and commitment.

Difficulties with intimacy may also be related to feelings of anger. As children, many of you were taught not to feel angry. Anger can be a healthy expression if verbalized in a productive way. To some of you, anger is an unfamiliar feeling. Many people feel angry but don't show it. They hold it in. Over the years, those suppressed angry feelings are all shoved away. To begin to recognize how angry you may be, means to get in touch with those feelings. However, stuffing them for so long can make it very scary to go there. The fear is that these feelings will overwhelm you, and you are afraid of your own reactions.

Communication will be a problem when there is a fear of anger. It will not allow for healthy relating. It may be fear of your own anger or that of your partner's. You may be afraid to express anger when in conflict for fear of what you might say or do. On the other hand, you may be afraid of your partner's anger for the same reasons. Acting on these thoughts or beliefs will not allow for open and honest communication. It is also a way of avoiding conflict as well as a way to create distance between you and your partner.

Holding on to your anger may also be a form of punishment. In some cases, if you hold on to your anger, you may withdraw in a quiet way but still feel angry. If your partner approaches you, it is likely you will push him or her away and refuse to talk about the issue involved.

Sometimes, it is easier to stay angry and withhold loving feelings. If this is a pattern, it is important to recognize if your behavior is related to your fear of being close. In the above examples, you are using unproductive behaviors that will not lead to a close intimate relationship with healthy and productive communication.

The areas covered in this chapter hopefully gave you a new and different perspective on relating. Think about your own personality and whether you fit into any of the ones described. Can you identify with the vignettes and the ways these couples relate?

The above examples will also help you clarify where you are and what direction you need to take. You are probably aware by now of the differences between communication that is reactive and responsive. Depending on your personality type, you will be able to recognize the areas in which you need to improve. You will also recognize whether you are more reactive than responsive. If you find yourself feeling that you are more reactive, you will need to learn how to relate differently. In the next chapter, this will be addressed. You will be able to begin changing your patterns.

Compatibility, as with personality types, will also enable you to be aware of the kinds of people you find attractive. You will become more aware of your patterns and whether or not they are repetitious. In addition, we know that if one person wants change in a relationship, it will upset the status quo, which will ultimately lead to changes in the relationship. The importance of how you express or don't express your anger plays an important part of communication. For good communication, it is important that all feelings be expressed. You may need to work through any feelings that you have trouble with in order to have direct and honest communication.

CHAPTER 10

Practice Makes Perfect

You are already aware that change is difficult in any area. Most people do not like change. Even positive change can bring about feelings of loss, anxiety, and discomfort. In making any changes, you will be losing something. In making new changes in your relationship, you are letting go of old behaviors and ways of relating. This will bring up a sense of loss. For most of you, you will find that you are giving up familiar patterns that have been comfortable for your entire life. These lifelong patterns have been instilled in you and your actions are predictable. Changing these lifelong patterns is very difficult and it takes a great deal of motivation and practice.

In making changes in your relationship, it is first important to recognize these old familiar patterns of relating. You may find yourself identifying with one or more of the personalities I described earlier, which will give you an idea about how you argue or resolve conflicts.

You must be able to recognize those patterns prior to thinking about making any new changes. It is also essential to begin setting goals for what you would like to see change. You want to begin to identify more positive ways of relating to make your relationship last. In addition, begin to ask yourself how and when the conflicts arose. What are the problems, and what is your part in creating them? What are both of you doing that is not working? It is also important to know your partner and to be able to understand their part and what their role has been in acting and encouraging destructive behaviors. Next it is important to begin looking at the options that are available to you, so that you are able to set realistic goals. If your goals are not realistic, you are only setting yourself up for more failure.

Once you have identified your goals and begin to look at the options available, you and your partner will need to decide what will work best for you. In addition, you need to decide whether you can make these changes using the knowledge and skills you have learned without professional help. You may feel that this is going to be too difficult to do alone and a third independent party might be helpful. In that case, it may be more productive to enter into marital counseling for guidance and direction. You would be able to practice your skills and have someone make suggestions that would be helpful and allow this process to move more quickly. However, that decision can be made at any time. If you are doing well by yourselves, you may want to continue that way. If you get stuck, you may want to consider getting help.

Resolution of your conflicts and issues will lead to a better and healthier relationship. Again, both of you must be motivated to change. However, motivation and change will come only if you are in a relationship in which there is love, respect, and commitment.

Once you begin to use your skills, changes will come about with practice. You will need to practice these skills over and over until communication in this new way feels natural and comfortable. When you get to that point, you will know that changed has occurred.

In previous chapters, you have learned ways of communicating that can be both productive and unproductive. Let's look at some other areas and exercises to help you further enhance your ways of relating.

The following is a list of different concepts that are the essentials for good communication. Examine your understanding of these concepts in order to help you begin to identify and to work on the conflicts in your relationship. In the previous chapter, reacting and responding was discussed. However, the importance of these two concepts can't be stressed enough, so they will be briefly discussed again in this chapter.

Reflective Listening: Are you really hearing what your partner said? Can you repeat what you heard in order to clarify the points being made? Reflective listening is when one is able to really hear what their partner is saying. They can reflect by repeating back what they heard. They may have heard it the way their partner meant it, or they may have to clarify what was being said in order to respond in a way where their partner feels heard.

Validation: If you can hear what your partner is saying, can you also feel what your partner is feeling? Can you feel it with empathy and understanding? Are you being loving, caring, accepting, and showing concern? Validation means respecting who your partner is.

It means that you are not judgmental and are able to relate and show that you understand in both a feeling and verbal way.

Honesty: In all interaction, honesty is crucial for a healthy relationship. The first step is being honest with yourself. You can't be honest with your partner unless you are honest with yourself. It means being real and direct about who you are. Honesty is a major part in all of your interactions. It means you are sincere, open; it means you tell the truth. Some people say what they think their partner wants to hear. Is that being honest or is that wanting to appease so you can avoid conflict? Honesty means you are able to tell your partner the positive and the negative. Most people try to avoid sharing negative thoughts, which may be considered as criticism. Honesty means you have learned to offer constructive criticism, so you can say what you feel without causing conflict.

Others are closed and will not share important feelings. They may be afraid of feeling too vulnerable if they are too open. Then there are others who feel they have to be honest about everything, which means sharing all. It's like the child who feels bad about him or herself and feels guilty about many of their actions. They feel to rid themselves of these bad feelings, they have to report everything to their parents. They know there will be consequences, but they think it's more important to be honest and tell it all. As adults, we don't have to share everything. Is that being dishonest or is that being wise? It may again be the child who feels the need to rid themselves of any guilt they feel. Sometimes, people go overboard. They feel if they don't share everything, then they are not being honest. However, that is not true. This is your partner, your equal, not your mother. You want to be honest but it is essential to separate your need to tell all and the need to be truthful. It is not necessary to report all. But if you do share you want to be honest about it. It is not necessary to share every conversation you had during the day, especially if it is not relevant to your relationship. You may want to share events of the day, which is different than saying things that might be hurtful. Why would you tell your partner someone flirted with you that day? Whose need is that? Your partner probably doesn't want to hear it and may feel you are trying to make him or her jealous.

Honesty means to be truthful, open, sincere, and loving in your communication, without a selfish need to share what may very well be inappropriate and possibly destructive.

Responding: Are you responding or reacting in you dialogue with your partner? Can you be specific and stick to one situation? Do you tell your partner how to feel? If your partner says they are feeling sad, don't tell them not to feel that way. There are no right or wrong to feelings; they just are. I am sure you have felt a certain way, and the last thing you want to hear is not to feel that way. Many parents react to their children in this manner. A child may feel physically hurt after falling and start to cry. Mother's reaction may be, "Stop crying, you really didn't hurt yourself." She could have responded by saying, "That really must have hurt. The hurt will go away soon."

In addition to responsive behaviors, again it is important to remember that there is no right or wrong to feelings. It is the behaviors that can be right or wrong. There are some behaviors that are inappropriate and do not warrant any validation. People need to observe their behaviors as well as recognize what they are doing. Some of these behaviors may have consequences.

It is also important to be aware if you are trying to outdo each other? If you are, you will bring out more hostile feelings. Sometimes, an argument will begin with a specific area. The argument may escalate. You are off the topic and into a power struggle trying to surpass each other in an area that has nothing to do with the original problem. You may also want to ask yourself if you are you using criticism in your communication? If one partner needs to talk about something, are you criticizing them for what they say, the problem they are talking about or who they are? In critical reactions, you are not responding. You are only bringing harm to the relationship. Are you someone who tries to outdo your partner in an argument? Are you being critical of your partner? If so, you are already aware of how destructive this can be.

Reacting: Reacting is the opposite of responding. When you react, you will most likely put your partner on the defensive. Your partner may take it as an attack and attack back. Reacting can be accusatory. And you will not receive a response that you want to hear. You may end up going back and forth in attacks. This is the most unproductive form of verbal communication.

It is important to take time in hearing your partner and then thinking what you want to say that would again show that you answering your partner in a way that shows validation. Responding is crucial. It incorporates most of good communication. It can prevent conflict into escalating and remaining unresolved. It is important to practice thinking what you say, or how you want to say it before you do it.

Respect: Respect is one of the key words used above and necessary in order to make changes in your relationship. Do you respect your partner? Do you respect their needs and differences even if they are not your own needs? Can you accept these needs? You may not fully understand their needs, but it is important that you allow your partner to have them. Respect will show that you care for and love your partner. As mentioned earlier, when we see differences between men and women. It is more important to respect these differences then to try and fully understand them.

Judy and Ted were having many problems in their marriage for a long time. It appears they grew up in chaotic, dysfunctional families, and now they have created their own.

One big issue had to do with Judy's need for time alone. Many times, Judy would come home from work in a terrible mood. She would go to her room and close the door. This was a trigger for Ted, as he thought he did something to upset her. His usual pattern would be to try and talk to her. He would try and get her to talk about what was bothering her. This only exacerbated Judy's mood making her feel angrier. Many times Judy was not aware of what was bothering her. She just knew that she felt angry about something. What Judy needed from Ted was to let her have this time alone. It wouldn't last for long, but she didn't want to talk with him or anyone. Judy was able to express this need to Ted. Although Ted did not understand her needs, he was willing to respect her needs as well as to accept them. This was difficult for Ted to do, as he felt the need to do something to make her feel better. However, respecting her wishes, which he didn't understand, he left her alone. The result was that Judy didn't have the need to stay away so long. She also felt loving towards Ted for giving her that space.

TRANSFERENCE

It is important to understand the unproductive use of displacement and transference in your relationship. One of the most common problems I have seen in the way couples relate to each other has to do with the theory of transference.

Displacement and transference are terms to describe how people place feelings and thoughts on to someone else that are really not relevant to that person. This can make for very dysfunctional communication. What happens is that when you get angry, you may speak to your partner by calling him or her names that have nothing to do with them. You may feel very angry with your partner, but what you are doing is transferring feelings and thoughts you may have had toward your mother and/or father. You bring your old negative feelings that you have towards a parent and displace it onto your partner.

Dennis came home from work one evening and began to pick a fight with Ellie. He was very angry and began yelling at her. Ellie started to feel just as angry, but also felt what he was saying didn't seem like he was upset with her. The accusations he made were not about things that she had done. Ellie realized that something wasn't right. She decided not to react to Dennis and let him yell until he was finished. Actually, she was very responsive to him, which helped calm him down. Ellie could have taken it personally and reacted toward him by yelling back. This way would have been unproductive. What was really going on was that Dennis was really angry with his mother. Unaware of his suppressed feelings of anger toward his mother, he believed he was angry with Ellie. Initially, Ellie would react, but after a while she began to recognize the displacement or transference of his feelings.

As a therapist, taking a good family history helps to understand the dynamics in the family of origin and the present relationship. Sometimes, when a couple is seen in therapy, there is a visualization of six people in the room—the couple and both sets of parents. It is not difficult to see in a session when a couple comes in angry whether or not they are really angry with their partner or this is truly a displacement or transference of feelings. Helping the person recognize what they are doing and why it is happening is a big step in beginning to stop that behavior. It is then important for the person who is displacing their feelings to work on the real issues and identify where the anger is coming from and why—you need to ask yourself where is the transference? With whom am I really angry and why is the anger being transferred to my partner?

"I" Statements and Assertive Communication: The previous chapter briefly discussed the use of "I" statements to improve your communication. "I" statements can really make a big difference in how you speak to your partner and how they respond. The basic idea of using this is to have responsive rather than reactive responses. To use "I" statements you will be getting across your point in an assertive manner without attacking and without beginning your sentence with "You." For example: "I feel angry because you did not call today which makes me feel disappointed."

You are talking about the way you feel because of your partner's behavior and then taking it back again to the way you feel. You will not see your partner reacting, attacking, or become defensive. Most likely your partner will respond to you.

Art: "Is dinner ready?"

Jackie: "I've just been too busy. Can't we go out?"

Art: "You're just plain lazy!"

Jackie: "Let's not talk about who's lazy!"

As you might guess this is not a productive interaction. After this dialogue, the couple probably left the room pouting and angry. You will notice, there was no respect or acceptance of what each one was saying or feeling. In addition, the conversation went from eating dinner to who's lazy. They also began to try and outdo each other, which as mentioned earlier, lead to more hostile feelings.

Jackie: "I feel angry when you accuse me of being lazy. It makes me feel very inadequate."

Art: "When I feel tired and hungry, I really want a home cooked meal. When you haven't made dinner, it makes me feel that I'm not important."

This is an example showing the use of "I" statements and assertive communication. They are both being honest and direct, staying on the subject, and saying what they feel without being reactive, defensive, or attacking.

"I" statements are essential for good communication not only with your partner but also as a general rule in all communication. The concept is being used to teach children as well as adults. It takes a great deal of practice. Practice is essential until you no longer have to give it much thought and it comes naturally. You will notice a difference in how you feel and the responses you receive. You will also notice a positive change in your relationship.

Absolutes: Never use absolutes during an argument. Always and never are examples of absolutes. When you use absolutes, you are talking about the past. You are not staying in the present and focusing on what the issue is that day. Absolutes lead to further arguments, misunderstandings, and resentments. They can lead you down a path different from the one you entered

George: "You never make dinner."

Jodi: "Yes I do."

George: "No you don't! You are always too busy with your own things."

Jodi: "You're always working! You're never home. Why should I cook when you're never around?"

The absolutes in the above example, which both partners use, are "never" and "always."

A more constructive dialogue for this couple would look like the following:

George: "I am really hungry. I hope you were able to make dinner."

Jodi: "I was so busy today, and I thought you would be coming home late."

George: "I know I should call you when I will be home late, and I promise to do so in the future."

Jodi: "Thank you. I will put together something now."

Negotiation and Compromise: I am sure you have heard "win-win," "win-lose," and "lose-lose" situations. It is obvious in a "win-win" situation that both partners win. In a "win-lose" situation, one partners wins, however that does not imply negotiation or compromise. It assumes that there is a power struggle and that only one person wins. However, they are not moving anywhere as far as resolution of a conflict. A "lose-lose" situation usually implies aggressive and hostile communication in which nothing gets resolved and the conflict remains. Here we are looking for "win-win" situations in which there is negotiation and compromise when disagreement begins to arise. The result will be mutually satisfying. Issues need to be discussed until you can come to an agreement that is mutually satisfying. It means give and take. It may necessitate that both have to give up certain behaviors. It may also mean that you will be asked to do things you don't really want to do. However, in return, you partner will be doing the same.

Pat: "I really don't want to go to the farm every weekend. I have so much to do around the house. If I weren't working, it would be different."

Andy: "You know how much I love the farm. I want us to spend as much time out there as we possible can."

Pat: "I know you love the farm. Can we try and work out a compromise that would meet both of our needs?"

Andy: "I suppose so. I just want you to know how much going there means to me."

Pat: "I do know. I think we can work something out."

Pat and Andy agreed to go out to the farm every other weekend and long holiday weekends. Andy would also go alone during his days off to work around the farm doing projects he enjoys.

Touching: Touching is crucial for a good relationship. Touching is a way of showing love and affection. It's a behavior that speaks without words. Touching can be in the form of a hug, or a pat. It can be anything that shows a positive physical interaction and does not require the other to necessarily reciprocate. Touching can also be used as a way to diffuse negative feelings. When a couple is talking to each other, touching can be a way to prevent a conversation from escalating into an argument. It is a very effective way of communicating.

Touching is also an expression of love and caring as part of sex. As mentioned earlier, being demonstrative in a way that is emotional and includes touch and pleasing one's partner will also lead to better communication. When both partners feel mutually involved while having sex, they are relating on more than one level. Too many issues arise if that is not the case. If sex is just the act of sex in which one person only derives pleasure, it can create conflicts. There is no doubt that the conflict arising in the bedroom will get displaced into others areas of conflict outside of the bedroom.

Some people feel that sex is the most important part of intimacy. That usually is not true. It becomes the most important part of the relationship when it does not exist, or when it exists as a selfish act. Good communication in which there is negotiation and compromise will carry over to the bedroom. The most common issue around sex is that it is a very sensitive area and can be difficult to approach. Two partners may view the situation differently. One area of difficulty can be the frequency of sex. As I said earlier, this might not be the case for all, but it is very common for men to want sex more than women. If this is the issue, it is imperative that you both compromise. You need to negotiate and compromise until you can come to an agreement that is satisfactory for both of you. You may try and vary the times that you have sex as well as be more spontaneous in a way that meets both of your schedules and needs. If your partner really wants to be more sexually active, it is possible to compromise in a way that he get his sexual needs met. You may then want to look at needs you have in other areas that you can ask him to meet. This is not easy, but with constant communication, you will eventually work out conflicts that will make you both happy.

Touching is a very important aspect of intimacy. Intimacy is made up of those components that connect two people. Touching, sex, communication are all a part of intimacy. If you think about it, what relationships do you know of that last? What do these two people have that many other couples are missing? It's not intimacy, but the mutual need for intimacy. If two people have the same needs for closeness, the relationship has a good chance for success. When your needs differ, this can bring about major conflicts, which need resolution. When needs are not the same, feelings of resentment toward your partner may emerge. This is a time that a relationship can go into crisis. This can be a very anxious time. At this time, one partner may be thinking about leaving the relationship. If you are in crisis, therapy is highly recommended to save the relationship.

Non-Verbal Behaviors: It is not difficult to tell how someone feels when you look at their face. Facial expression can sometimes say more than words. Faces express joy, sadness, anger, hurt, and other feelings. If you are saying something to your partner, you may begin to tell immediately, by their facial expressions, how they are feeling at that moment. It may even change the direction you are going as a response to what your partner may be feeling. It can show how open your partner is to listening to you, whether or not they are feeling tense or relaxed. Looking at body language is a good clue to what your partner may be feeling and a very helpful tool for better communication. You can tell from the way a person sits, stands, has their arms or legs positioned how they may be feeling. There are times when non verbal cues can give you more awareness of your partner's feeling than if they just talked. Sometimes, nonverbal communication is more honest, especially if your partner has difficulty expressing feelings or being direct in their communication.

The above concepts, techniques, and examples will give you the essential tools for a more productive way of communicating. You must emphasize the importance of practice. You can begin by practicing alone or with your partner. Do what feels the most comfortable for you. However, as you gain better understanding, you will need to practice with your partner. Each concept presented must be understood in order to practice. If it is confusing, which it shouldn't be, then you need to really look closer until you have a good grasp on what it is you are trying to learn. Talking about these concepts until you both feel you are comfortable is the first step. Then comes the practice.

Role-playing is a great way to practice. You can role-play by having each of you pretend you are someone else. You can choose a topic to discuss or possibly act out a scenario. An example would be an argument between two other people. It might be you and your partner pretending that you are your partner's parents. You are arguing and you play out that argument as if you both were his parents. You may act as you think they would. Another example would be to reverse roles. You take on the role of your partner and he or she becomes you. Choose a topic and talk to each other as you believe you would interact.

As you keep role-playing, it begins to feel more natural. Reminding each other when negative feelings emerge, that you are not doing something right. Go back and review the area that is causing the problem. This is also a good way to avoid negative escalation between the two of you. It's a way of diverting the content back to the concept.

With constant practice, you will feel more comfortable. You will soon begin to see changes in your way of relating. You will begin to feel more connected in a positive way. Your relationship will become more satisfying.

CHAPTER **11**

The Blueprint of the Whole Shoot'n Match

This book has given you the necessary tools to make the changes that will bring you closer to having a successful relationship. To use these tools, it is important to work on a plan. The purpose is to develop a framework from which you can work. It will help clarify where you begin and where you end. It will make it easier for you to begin to make changes.

The following is a list of steps that you can use as an outline. The outline will provide examples.

Recognize Your Patterns.

Identify the Changes You Want to Make.

Set Your Goals.

Develop a Plan of Action.

Implement Your Plan.

RECOGNIZING YOUR PATTERNS

You may now be aware of the patterns you see in your relationships. However, it still may be difficult to recognize your own patterns. These are the patterns that have caused you problems. You must first begin to look at your repetitious behaviors in your relationships. As mentioned earlier, your patterns may stem from childhood experiences. However, some of you may not remember or may not have a clear picture of your family dynamics during that time. It may be easier to start from the present and work backwards.

First ask yourself if you are able to identify with any of the examples given in the book? If so, try to think of your patterns that were familiar and repetitious. If not, begin by looking at your last few relationships. Think about any similarities in the partners you chose. They may have been very different people, but there might be a common thread. Did the relationships begin the same way; did they end in the same way?

If you are someone who dates for a while and terminates the relationships after two to six months, you will see an established pattern. Hopefully from reading this book, you will understand why this happens. If not, at least you know that you have a pattern you may want to change.

Maybe you fall in love too soon. The chemistry is there and you get involved. The relationship doesn't last and you realize that you are dating someone who is not emotionally available. How many times have you done this? You probably have had this happen more than once. That is a pattern that you want to recognize as a problem.

You think you want to be in a close and committed relationship. When you get to a point where your partner wants more of a commitment, you can't make one. You are too ambivalent. One of you ends the relationship. It is not the first time this has happened. This is another pattern you can recognize.

You are looking for the perfect person. You are now in your forties and haven't found him or her. There is a pattern there in which you find things wrong with your partners. They don't meet your expectations. Ask yourself if your expectations are realistic; is there a pattern of fear running through this theme?

You and your partner argue too much. There is no real communication. You recognize this has been a pattern soon after you began your relationship. You are able to see that the relationship is not moving forward in a healthy way.

These are some examples of patterns. They are patterns because they repeat themselves. If you are not in a satisfying relationship, it is important to begin to recognize your patterns and carefully look at your history. If you don't think you have any patterns but your relationships don't work, you can assume you have them. You may be able to see them by exploring all your relationships looking for repeated behaviors. You need to go back through your history. You need to begin to question your behavior or your partner's behavior if they made you unhappy. Ask yourself how you got into this relationship.

What was appealing about your partner? What was not appealing about your partner? Why did you end the relationship? Why did he or she end it? You also have to delve into your family history. What were the members of your family like? How did they interact? How did they make you feel as a person? Were your emotional needs being met? Did you see yourself as a happy child? Were you sad, angry, disappointed much of the time? What did you want and need from your parents? These are just examples to give you the means to look at patterns and be able to recognize the issues you may have and want to change.

IDENTIFYING THE CHANGES YOU WANT TO MAKE

In order to identify the changes you want to make, you must complete the above step of recognizing your patterns. You must be able to clearly state what your patterns are. You also must understand how these patterns emerged. You will be unable to identify any changes you want to make without a clear understanding of your history, and how out of that history you will recognize the problems you have with relationships. You need to be able to answer the following questions:

What are my problems with relationships?

How have these problems interfered with a successful relationship?

How have my childhood relationships played a part in these issues?

What were my parents' roles in contributing to bad relationships?

How did my entire family dynamics play a role?

Did I have peer group influence that made my issues worse?

Below are some areas that you may relate to and list in identifying the changes you wish to make. In order for any changes to take place, you need to make a major commitment to change and follow this outline in-depth.

You have a pattern of being noncommittal in all your relationships. You now want to change that because you feel you want to be in a long-term committed relationship.

You keep picking unavailable men or women. These relationships cause you to feel insecure and anxious. You want someone who will be able to love and commit to you. You want to begin choosing available partners.

You want to get married. However, you can't find the perfect person. You recognize that your pattern isn't working for you. You would like to change your criteria and beliefs about a potential partner.

You want your relationship to work. However, the lack of good communication has been destructive to your relationship. You recognize that your patterns of relating need to change. You want to change some of the ways you communicate with your partner.

You are able to recognize that you are afraid of being close in a relationship. As a result you have terminated relationships. You now want to work through your fears so you can allow yourself to feel close with your partner.

SETTING GOALS

Your goals are what you would like to see happen. Ask yourself how the entire picture would look once you have met your goals. Your goals will stem from the first two steps of recognizing your patterns and identifying the changes you want to make. You may think that your goal would be to have a good relationship. That is an overall goal. To achieve your overall goal, you must begin with smaller goals that are specific and realistic. If you achieve your smaller goals, it will lead to your overall goal of having a good relationship. You want to set goals that you can accomplish. Some examples of goals that you might have would be:

To be less fearful and avoidant of closeness.

To be able to commit to my partner.

To avoid an emotionally unavailable partner.

To choose a partner who may not be perfect but just right.

To be less critical and more open to a healthy partner.

To be less dependent on my partner.

To have better communication with my partner.

To work through my unresolved grief.

To change my belief system about men or women.

To overcome fears of intimacy and commitment.

These are a list of some specific goals. They may be part of your list or you may have goals that are not on the list. Again, be specific and realistic so you don't fail. If you have some of the above goals, you may not be able to achieve these goals without help. Some of them are more complex. They will require a deeper understanding of your dynamics and will necessitate professional help.

DEVELOPING A PLAN OF ACTION

This part requires that you take your list of goals and develop a plan on how you will meet those goals. This is the plan that you will put into action in the next step.

This step will require a lot of thought, because these are the actions that you will be executing. Your plan also needs to be behavioral and specific. Some examples might include:

I will talk about my fear of intimacy and commitment with my partner once week.

I will read over the chapter in this book on fears of intimacy and commitment weekly.

If necessary, I will begin therapy on a weekly basis alone or with my partner.

I will become less dependent on my partner by spending two evenings a week with my friends.

I will find one new interest that doesn't include my partner. I will take a class on improving my self-esteem.

I will watch out for early signs that indicate my partner is emotionally unavailable.

I will end a relationship with an emotionally unavailable partner as soon as I see the same patterns that I have had with other unavailable partners.

I will only date someone who is available.

I will give a relationship several months before I make any decisions.

I will be aware of the possibility of my own need for distancing and recognize my own issues with intimacy and commitment.

I will not end the relationship if my partner becomes boring, feels suffocating, or pays too much attention to me.

If you have difficulty tolerating someone who is available and want to end the relationship, it may mean that you are at an anxious and uncomfortable point. You want to run, but don't. Getting past the above issues may give you the chance to finally get close to someone. If you stay with someone who is nice, after a while, the relationship can get comfortable You may become more attached than you realized.

My partner and I will review the chapters in this book on communication. We will review all the concepts reading that chapter twice a week for one month until we are comfortable with the methods.

My partner and I will practice communication skills three times a week for several months.

After my divorce, I will not get into a relationship until I have worked through my issues around the divorce. I will surround my self with friends and family several times a week. I will talk about my sadness, my anger, and my feelings of abandonment once a week.

IMPLEMENTING YOUR PLAN

You have recognized your patterns, identified the changes you want to make, set your goals, and developed a plan of action.

This step involves taking your plan of action and doing it. It is the action phase of this process. It is at this part of the process where you follow through with new thinking and behaviors—this is the most difficult part. It may be scary and uncomfortable. Hopefully, you are committed to give it your best effort. It means a great deal of work and persistence.

At this point, you probably have a good understanding of what you need in order to have a successful relationship. You may still feel doubtful, as that is how you felt when you began reading this book. However, if you have absorbed all the information chapter by chapter, relationships will hopefully take on a new meaning for you. You should be able to take a good look at yourself and have the ability to understand and reflect upon your own experiences. These experiences are the key to opening the door to new and different ways of perceiving yourself and your behavior in relationships.

It is possible to achieve your goals. All it takes is the desire, motivation, and practice to get there. Many people have had difficulty with relationships. They believed nothing would ever change. However, with the knowledge, insight, and skill provided in this book, they were able to obtain a satisfying, healthy relationship. All that you need to take that road to happiness is right in front of you. You will find that it is possible to have a long lasting, satisfying relationship. You may just beat the odds that were against you in this game of "relationship roulette."

For Further Reading

Feel the Fear . . . and Do It Anyway,
by Susan Jeffers, Ph.D. (Ballantine, 2007)

Love Is Not Enough: What It Takes to Make It Work,
by Henry Kellerman, Ph.D. (Praeger, 2009)

Men Who Hate Women and the Women Who Love Them: When Loving Hurts and You Don't Know Why,
by Susan Forward, Ph.D., and Joan Torres (Bantam, 2002)

Receiving Love: Transform Your Relationship By Letting Yourself Be Loved,
by Harville Hendrix, Ph.D., and Helen LaKelly Hunt, Ph.D. (Atria, 2004)

The Relationship Cure: A 5 Step Guide to Strengthening Your Marriage, Family, and Friendships,
by John M. Gottman, Ph.D. (Crown, 2001)

The Seven Principles for Making Marriage Work: A Practical Guide from the Country's Foremost Relationship Expert,
by John M. Gottman, Ph.D., and Nan Silver (Crown, 1999)

Smart Women Foolish Choices: Finding the Right Men Avoiding the Wrong Ones,
by Connell Cowan, Ph.D., and Melvyn Kinder, Ph.D. (Penguin, 1986)

Index

About the Author

CAROL DIAMOND COHEN, a native New Yorker, has been a licensed practicing psychotherapist for 25 years working with individuals and couples. She earned her M.S.W. at the University of Missouri and has lectured widely, conducting seminars and workshops on relationships, and relationship building. Carol presently lives in the Philadelphia area with her husband.